OHIO STUDIES IN PERSONNEL

Leader Behavior: Its Description and Measurement

Edited by
Ralph M. Stogdill
and
Alvin E. Coons

RESEARCH MONOGRAPH NUMBER 88
BUREAU OF BUSINESS RESEARCH
THE OHIO STATE UNIVERSITY

LEADER BEHAVIOR:
ITS DESCRIPTION AND MEASUREMENT

LEADER BEHAVIOR:
ITS DESCRIPTION AND MEASUREMENT

Edited By
Ralph M. Stogdill
and
Alvin E. Coons

Published by
THE BUREAU OF BUSINESS RESEARCH
COLLEGE OF COMMERCE AND ADMINISTRATION
THE OHIO STATE UNIVERSITY
COLUMBUS 10, OHIO

COLLEGE OF COMMERCE AND ADMINISTRATION
WALTER C. WEIDLER, *Dean*

BUREAU OF BUSINESS RESEARCH STAFF
VIVA BOOTHE, *Director*

JAMES C. YOCUM, *Marketing*
MIKHAIL V. CONDOIDE, *Economics*
PAUL G. CRAIG, *Economics*
RALPH M. STOGDILL, *Personnel*
OMAR GOODE, *Tabulations*

Research Assistants

EYVONNE COCHRAN
MARY PRIEST MARTIN
MARTHA N. STRATTON
JAYANTILAL SANGHVI
WILLIAM D. OYLER
MARTHA MOUNTS, *Assistant to the Director*

THE OHIO STATE UNIVERSITY

PERSONNEL RESEARCH BOARD

*BOOTHE, VIVA, *Professor and Director, Bureau of Business Research*
BOWERS, EDISON L., *Professor of Economics and Chairman of Department*
BURTT, HAROLD E., *Professor of Psychology and Chairman of Department*
CORNELL, MERRISS, *Associate Professor, School of Social Administration*
FAWCETT, HAROLD P., *Professor of Education and Chairman of Department*
FLETCHER, FRANK M., JR., *Professor of Psychology and Director, University Counseling and Testing Center*
*FORSHAY, ARTHUR W., *Professor of Education; Director, Bureau of Educational Research*
GREEN, ROBERT S., *Executive Director, Engineering Experiment Station*
HOWLAND, DANIEL, *Assistant Professor, Industrial Engineering*
JUCIUS, MICHAEL J., *Professor, Department of Business Organization*
MANSFIELD, HARVEY C., *Professor of Political Science and Chairman of Department*
*SHARTLE, CARROLL L., *Professor of Psychology; Chairman, Personnel Research Board*
*SLETTO, RAYMOND F., *Professor of Sociology and Chairman of Department*
SMITH, MERVIN G., *Professor of Agricultural Economics and Rural Sociology and Chairman of Department*

*Executive Committee

COPYRIGHT, 1957
By
THE OHIO STATE UNIVERSITY

FOREWORD

There are described in this monograph the procedures involved in the development of a research tool, the Leader Behavior Description Questionnaire; the successive revisions and adaptations of the questionnaire; and summaries of the results of its use in a variety of organizational settings.

The work here reported involved many investigators working at The Ohio State University over a period of years. These workers with their present professional connections are identified with the section of this report for which each was primarily responsible.

This monograph is one of the Leadership Series in Ohio Studies in Personnel published by the Bureau of Business Research as a part of the Bureau's participation in the research program of the Personnel Research Board.

A list of the nine monographs in the Leadership Series, with a brief description of each study, is given in Appendix C.

VIVA BOOTHE, *Director*
Bureau of Business Research

PREFACE

The Ohio State Leadership studies represent an interdisciplinary undertaking. The major contributors were psychologists, sociologists and economists. An interdisciplinary approach was not interpreted to require that all projects use the same methods. However, one instrument was used in common by all investigators. This was the Leader Behavior Description Questionnaire, originated by Hemphill and expanded as the result of a large scale, cooperative effort.

The Leader Behavior Description Questionnaire has been administered in a wide variety of situations. It has been used for the study of the commanders and crew members of bomber crews in the Department of the Air Force; commissioned officers, noncommissioned personnel and civilian administrators in the Department of the Navy; foremen in a manufacturing plant; executives in regional cooperative associations; college administrators; school superintendents, principals and teachers; and leaders in a wide variety of student and civilian groups and organizations. Successive adaptations and revisions were made in the process of using the questionnaire.

The editors appreciate the opportunity to bring together a series of papers which tell at least part of the story of the group endeavor. It is their hope that the authors of the various papers will pardon the severe cutting and pruning they have done in order to reduce the size of the monograph to reasonable proportions.

It would be difficult to name individually all the persons who have made valuable contributions to the development and use of the LBDQ, and to the exploration of the concept of leadership in the over-all program. The work reported in this monograph received valuable support from a number of organizations. Among these are the Air Force Personnel and Training Research Center, Department of the Air Force; the Office of Naval Research, Department of the Navy; the Rockefeller Foundation; International Harvester Company; the Kellogg Foundation; the Ohio Farm Bureau

Cooperative Wholesale; Indiana Farm Bureau Cooperative Wholesale; Midland Cooperative Wholesale; Central Cooperative Wholesale; and The Ohio State University Research Foundation.

Ralph M. Stogdill
Alvin E. Coons

TABLE OF CONTENTS

Section Number		Page
I.	Introduction	1
	Carroll L. Shartle	
II.	Development of the Leader Behavior Description Questionnaire	6
	John K. Hemphill and Alvin E. Coons	
III.	A Factorial Study of the Leader Behavior Descriptions	39
	Andrew W. Halpin and B. James Winer	
IV.	The Leader Behavior and Effectiveness of Aircraft Commanders	52
	Andrew W. Halpin	
V.	The Observed Leader Behavior and Ideal Leader Behavior of Aircraft Commanders and School Superintendents	65
	Andrew W. Halpin	
VI.	Leader Behavior and Group Characteristics	69
	Carl H. Rush, Jr.	
VII.	Leader Behavior Associated with the Administrative Reputations of College Departments	74
	John K. Hemphill	
VIII.	A Comparison of General and Specific Leader Behavior Descriptions	86
	Melvin Seeman	
IX.	A Leader Behavior Description for Industry	103
	Edwin A. Fleishman	
X.	The Leadership Opinion Questionnaire	120
	Edwin A. Fleishman	
XI.	Leadership Opinion and Related Characteristics of Salesmen and Sales Managers	134
	Bernard M. Bass	
XII.	A Factorial Study of Very Short Scales	140
	Ralph M. Stogdill, William E. Jaynes and Ellis L. Scott	
Appendix A.	List of Items in the Leader Behavior Description Questionnaire: (Original Form of 150 Items)	153
Appendix B.	Item Analysis Data for 150 Items	159
Appendix C.	Annotated List of Monographs in the Leadership Series in Ohio Studies in Personnel	165

LIST OF TABLES

Section
and
Table
Number   Page

II. *Development of the Leader Behavior Description Questionnaire*.. 6

  1. Description of 205 Leaders by Subordinates: Intercorrelation between Dimension Scores and Their Correlation with Other Variables, Reliabilities, Means and Standard Deviations...... 22

  2. Self-Descriptions of 152 Leaders: Intercorrelations Between Dimension Scores and Their Correlation with Other Variables, Reliabilities, Means and Standard Deviations........... 23

  3. Centroid Factor Loadings of Leader Behavior Description Dimensions—Descriptions Made by Subordinates............ 24

  4. Centroid Factor Loadings of Leader Behavior Description Dimensions—Descriptions Made by the Leader of Himself... 25

III. *A Factorial Study of Leader Behavior Descriptions*............... 39

  1. Intercorrelations Among Eight Dimension Keys............. 40

  2. Distribution of Communalities for 130 Items................ 41

  3. Per Cent of Common Variance Accounted for by Four Factors.. 41

  4. Items With High Loadings on Factor I: Consideration....... 42

  5. Items With High Loadings on Factor II: Initiating Structure.. 42

  6. Items With High Loadings on Factor III: Production Emphasis 43

  7. Items With High Loadings on Factor IV: Sensitivity........ 44

  8. Intercorrelations of "Pure" and "Complex" Keys for Consideration and Initiating Structure: Reliability Coefficients for an Independent Sample of 100 Combat Aircrews............... 46

  9. Consideration Key: Factor Loadings Derived From 130-Item Form 47

  10. Initiating Structure Key: Factor Loadings Derived from 130-Item Form 48

  11. Analysis of Variance of Consideration Scores of 29 Air Crew Commanders Described by 201 Crew Members.............. 49

  12. Analysis of Variance of Initiating Structure Scores of 29 Air Crew Commanders Described by 201 Crew Members....... 49

  13. Correlations and Partial Correlations Between Effectiveness Ratings by Superiors and Leader Behavior Descriptions by Subordinates for 29 Air Crew Commanders................. 50

LIST OF TABLES—Continued

Section and Table Number		Page
IV.	*The Leader Behavior and Effectiveness of Aircraft Commanders*..	52
	1. Correlations Between Ascribed Consideration and Initiating Structure Scores and Ratings of Commanders by Superiors, and by Crew Members with Means and Standard Deviations For the Respective Variables..............................	59
	2. Correlations of Variables in Crew Acceptance Cluster with Factor Scores Derived from Superiors' Ratings of Aircraft Commanders	62
	3. Relation Between Consideration and Initiating Structure Scores of Aircraft Commanders Rated High or Low in Effectiveness by Superiors	63
	4. Number of Aircraft Commanders Scoring High or Low in Effectiveness and Scoring Above the Mean or Below the Mean in Both Leader Behavior Dimensions......................	63
V.	*The Observed Leader Behavior and Ideal Leader Behavior of Aircraft Commanders and School Superintendents*...........	65
	1. Means, Standard Deviations, and t Ratios of Mean Differences in Leader Behavior of 64 Administrators and 132 Commanders	66
	2. Correlations Among Descriptions of "Real" and "Ideal" Leader Behavior for 64 Administrators and 132 Commanders........	67
VI.	*Leader Behavior and Group Characteristics*.....................	69
	1. Correlation Between Leader Behavior Dimension Scores and Group Dimension Scores.................................	70
VII.	*Leader Behavior Associated With the Administrative Reputations of College Departments*..................................	74
	1. Average Scores on Consideration and Initiating Structure of Department Chairmen as Described by the Department Members	78
	2. Correlation Coefficients Expressing the Relationship Between the Administrative "Reputation" Scores of 18 College Departments and Four Leadership Scores of the Department Chairmen as Described by Department Members..................	80
	3. The Relationship Between the "Reputation" Achieved by College Departments and the Consideration and Initiating Structure Scores of 18 Department Chairmen.....................	81
	4. Correlation Between Each of Thirteen Group Dimensions (Average Scores) and Departments' Reputation for Being Well Administered	82

LIST OF TABLES—Continued

Section
and
Table
Number   Page

VIII. *A Comparison of General and Specific Leader Behavior Descriptions*   86

    1. Background Characteristics of Matched Samples Using General and Specific Leader Behavior Description Scales............ 89

    2. Comparison, on Six Rating Scale Measures, of Matched Samples Using General and Specific Leader Behavior Description Scales 90

    3. Intercorrelation Among Four Specific Leader Behavior Description Scales (n = 71)............................... 92

    4. Correlations Between Two Types of Leader Behavior Description Scales and Three Types of Self-Report Variables (n = 71) 96

    5. Bartlett's Chi Square Test for Homogeneity of Variance, and Analysis of Variance Among Nine Communities, for Initiating Structure and Consideration Scales (n = 63)................ 97

    6. Bartlett's Chi Square Test for Homogeneity of Variance, and Analysis of Variance Among Nine Communities, for Four Specific Leader Behavior Description Scales (n = 63)........ 98

IX. *A Leader Behavior Description for Industry*.................... 103

    1. Intercorrelations and Reliabilities of the Pre-Test Supervisory Behavior Description Dimension Scores (n = 100)........... 105

    2. Items Selected for the Revised Form of the Supervisory Behavior Description 108

    3. Means, Standard Deviations, Range, Reliabilities, and Intercorrelations of the Dimension Scores in the Revised Supervisory Behavior Description............................. 110

    4. Summary of Internal Consistency Reliabilities Obtained with the Supervisory Behavior Description from Various Samples..... 111

    5. Summary of Inter-Rates Agreement Coefficients Obtained with the Supervisory Behavior Description from Various Samples.. 111

    6. Summary of the Test-Retest Reliability Coefficients Obtained with the Supervisory Behavior Description from Various Samples 112

    7. Correlations Between the Supervisory Behavior Dimensions and Various Industrial Criteria of Leadership Effectiveness.. 114

    8. Correlations of Supervisory Behavior Dimensions with Other Measures for ROTC Cadets............................... 115

    9. Means and Standard Deviations of Supervisory Behavior Description Scores 116

LIST OF TABLES—Continued

Section and Table Number

X. The Leadership Opinion Questionnaire 120

    1. Items Selected for the Revised Form of the Leadership Opinion Questionnaire Key 122

    2. Means, Standard Deviations, Range, Reliabilities, and Intercorrelation of the Dimension Scores in the Revised Leadership Opinion Questionnaire 124

    3. Summary of Internal Consistency Reliabilities Obtained with the Leadership Opinion Questionnaire for Various Samples ... 125

    4. Test-Retest Reliability Coefficients Obtained With the Leadership Opinion Questionnaire 125

    5. Correlations Between Dimension Scores on the Leadership Opinion Questionnaire for Various Samples 126

    6. Correlations Between the Leadership Opinion Questionnaire Dimensions and Various Criteria 127

    7. Correlations of Leadership Opinion Questionnaire Dimensions and Various Psychometric and Other Measures 129

    8. Means and Standard Deviations of Leadership Opinion Questionnaire Scores for Various Samples 131

XI. Leadership Opinions and Related Characteristics of Salesmen and Sales Managers 134

    1. Leader Behavior Scores Correlated With Personal Characteristics and Performance Ratings 136

    2. Correlations Between Leadership Dimension Scores and Psychological Test Scores 138

XII. A Factorial Study of Very Short Scales 140

    1. Intercorrelations Among Leader Behavior Dimension Scores of 42 Officers on a Cruiser 141

    2. Intercorrelations Among Leader Behavior Dimension Scores of 33 Officers in a Naval Command Staff 141

    3. Factor Loadings Derived from Analysis of Tables 1 and 2 142

    4. Intercorrelations Among Leadership Measures in a Research Organization 143

    5. Intercorrelations Among Leadership Measures in Landing Ships (LST) 144

    6. Final Rotated Factor Loadings for Two Samples: LST's and Research Organization 145

LIST OF FIGURES

Page

Figure 1—Paradigm for the Study of Leadership...................... 3

I

INTRODUCTION

CARROLL L. SHARTLE
The Ohio State University

In the Ohio State Leadership Studies the approach to the topic of leadership has been that of examining and measuring performance or behavior rather than human traits. The trait approach had reached an impasse before the beginning of World War II. This may have been one of the reasons why leadership *per se* received relatively little emphasis as a research problem during the War. The topic was considered of very great importance by research planners, but the overwhelming emphasis of personnel research was concerned with other matters.

The Ohio State Leadership Studies, which have involved the efforts of several disciplines, had as one of their principal objectives the testing of hypotheses concerning the situational determination of leader behavior.

It was hypothesized that performance in a position of leadership is determined in a large part by demands made upon the position. This and related sub-hypotheses were accompanied by hypotheses concerning the variables that are important in a study of leadership. On the basis of practical experience and the analysis of previous research, it was hypothesized that status, work performance, personal interactions, responsibility, authority and personal behavior patterns constituted a minimum set of variables necessary for a study of leadership in organized groups. These hypotheses were not systematized so as to form a theoretical system. They served primarily to give direction to the research, to define the variables to be investigated, and to suggest methods of measurement.

When the Ohio State Leadership Studies were initiated in 1945, no satisfactory theory or definition of leadership was available. In spite of the lack of a satisfactory definition, it was decided that "leadership" should not be regarded as synonymous with "good leadership." This distinction has an important bearing on the criterion problem and on the design of leadership studies in general. When research is designed around the implicit assumption that only "good" leadership is leadership, the experimental variable is attenuated and so is the criterion. Therefore, it was decided to study leadership, however defined, and whether effective or ineffective.

Another important decision involved the nature and priority of the criterion of effectiveness. It was decided (1) that description and evaluation should be conducted as separate research operations, and (2) that description should precede evaluation. Why this departure from the traditional way of conducting a leadership study? First, one may ask, "If the nature and structure of leadership (i.e., the variables that describe it) are not known, how does one determine the relevance of a proposed criterion?" The fact that a composite criterion, the structure of which is not known, may show a high correlation with a composite predictor the structure of which is not known, does not greatly increase one's understanding of the variables being investigated. The utilitarian pressure for improved predictive measures without the basic knowledge necessary to improve prediction had already proved to be ineffective. If progress was to be made, it seemed necessary to learn something about the nature of leadership before trying to predict it. In actual practice in the Ohio State Leadership Studies, description and evaluation were often carried out simultaneously, but it was considered desirable to separate them both theoretically and procedurally.

The papers in this monograph are thus largely concerned with methods of describing leader behavior, or at least the behavior of persons placed in positions of high leadership potential. Criteria of relative goodness or poorness are reported in some cases. However, within the framework of the studies these evaluations are not the major consideration.

Figure 1 shows a paradigm for the study of leadership. It is a modified version of the original model which was initiated by the leadership studies group and prepared for publication by Morris and Seeman (1). It is noted that Leader Behavior Descrip-

FIGURE 1—Paradigm for the Study of Leadership

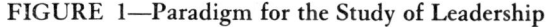

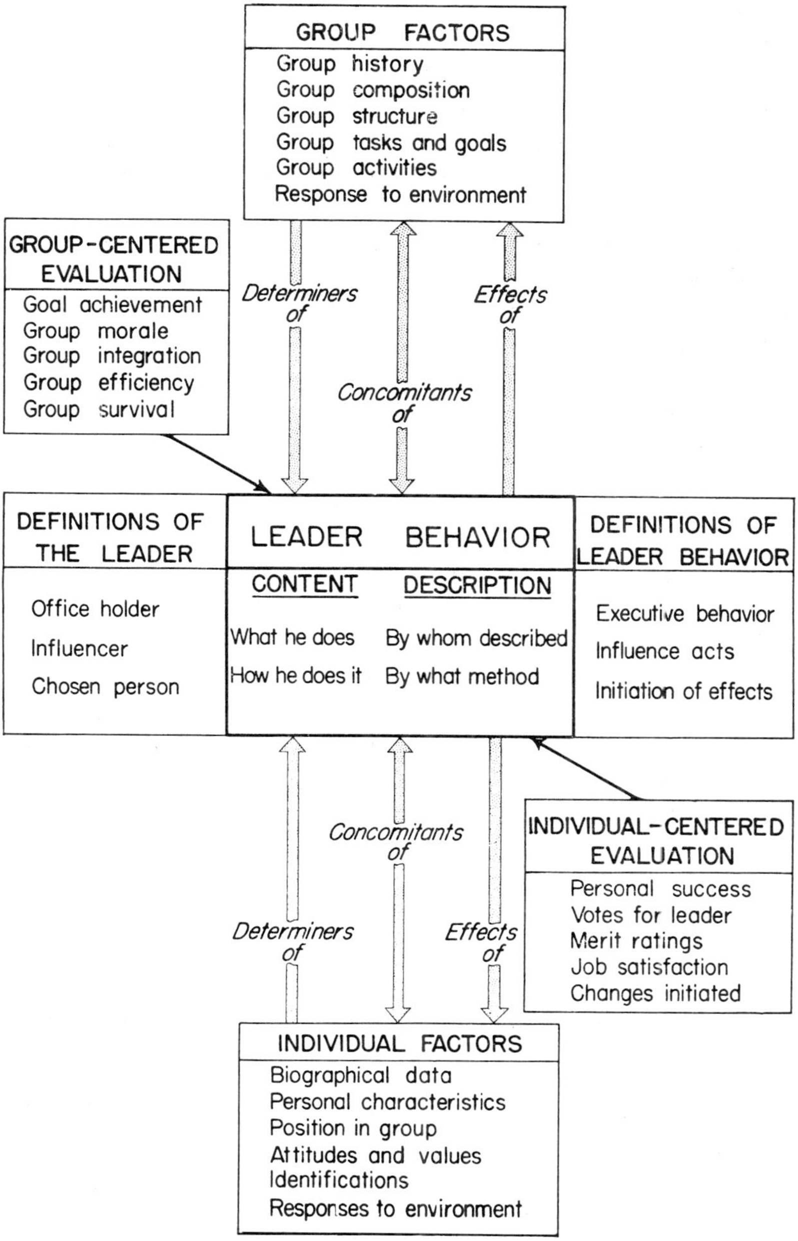

tion is the central point. Leader behavior may be concomitant with group factors such as history or group composition; and also concomitant with individual factors such as biographical data and personal characteristics. Likewise, the relationships between leader behavior and these factors may be in terms of effects or determiners. Evaluation may be group-centered or individual-centered. Not only is major research required on evaluation but likewise much research is needed on the individual and group factors that may help explain why an individual leads or attempts to lead the way he does.

Leader behavior as a focal point was the concern of everyone in the Ohio State Leadership Studies. Fortunately, it was something that was tackled by the staff in a straightforward fashion rather than something everyone was interested in but no one did anything about, as is sometimes the case in a large venture.

The following papers do not attempt to give final answers to the matter of describing leader behavior. However, it would seem that the descriptive dimensions represent useful concepts that are pertinent to research and to the utilization of research results.

The first paper in this monograph by Hemphill and Coons describes the initial stages in the development of the leader behavior description questionnaires, using nine hypothesized dimensions. Halpin and Winer then present a factorial study in which two dimensions of leader behavior emerge. This is followed by two papers by Halpin in which the dimensions are applied to military and school settings.

Rush reports the relationship between leader behavior dimension scores and group dimension scores in Air Force crews. Hemphill describes the use of the scales in studying departments in a liberal arts college.

Seeman, who studied school systems, reviews his findings and gives a comparison of general and specific leader behavior descriptions.

Fleishman, in the next two papers, takes the leader behavior dimensions to an industrial setting. He also reports further results from military samples.

Bass presents data from industry comparing leader behavior dimensions with certain test scores and other measures.

In the last paper Stogdill, Jaynes, and Scott describe a factorial study of very short leader behavior scales in which the two principal dimensions again emerge.

REFERENCES

1. Morris, Richard T. and Seeman, Melvin. The Problem of Leadership: An Interdisciplinary Approach. *Amer. J. Sociology,* 1950, *56,* 149–155.

II

DEVELOPMENT OF THE LEADER BEHAVIOR DESCRIPTION QUESTIONNAIRE

JOHN K. HEMPHILL, *Educational Testing Service*
ALVIN E. COONS, *The Ohio State University*

One segment of the study of leadership may be viewed as that of observing the behavior of individuals who have, by some specified criterion, been designated "leaders." To study the behavior of leaders thus designated, two approaches may prove useful. Framed as questions, they can be stated: (1) *What* does an individual do while he operates as a leader, and (2) *How* does he go about what he does?

The first approach was used in a series of studies undertaken by the Personnel Research Board at the outset in its program of research in the field of "Leadership in a Democracy." An attempt was made to determine the proportion of a leader's time spent in various individual and interpersonal activities, his level of responsibility and authority, and the like. The methods and results of these studies have been described by Shartle, Stogdill and associates (2, 3).

This report is concerned with an attempt to develop an objective method for describing *how* a leader carries out his activities. For example, a leader in his coordinating or supervisory activity, may engage in a considerable amount of dominating behavior; or, he may accomplish these tasks without displaying dominating behavior at all. To supplement the earlier studies, it was decided to explore the possibilities of using this second approach in designing an instrument to be used in describing leader behavior. Previous work by Hemphill (1) provided a start in this direction.

An introduction to the research described herein would be incomplete without mention of the interdisciplinary atmosphere within which it was carried on. An important motivation for the development of a method to describe how a leader behaves was the need felt by the staff of the Personnel Research Board for the coordination of individual research activities. In group discussions, it had become apparent that a major core of interest common to all individual research activities of the staff members lay in *how* a leader carried out his activities. It was decided, therefore, to make the development of a leader description instrument oriented toward "how he does it" a common task of the research staff.

It was agreed that the instrument should be adaptable to studies in widely different frames of reference. This would make it possible to include such an instrument in each individual research design, thereby contributing to an integration of research findings that would not be possible otherwise. Accordingly, development of the research tool to be described was undertaken by means of a process of group discussion, and decision, in a staff made up of psychologists, sociologists, and economists. Emphasis throughout was on the comparative development of a research instrument.

SPECIFICATION OF AREAS OF LEADER BEHAVIOR

Two major problems were encountered in the attempt to describe *how* a leader operates. The first concerned the problem of isolating that part of total behavior of an individual to be designated as leader behavior. The second was the problem of classification within this broad area.

A working definition of leadership had already been adopted as a part of the earlier studies in this field. Leadership, as tentatively defined, is the behavior of an individual when he is directing the activities of a group toward a shared goal. This definition points to behavior which can be called leader behavior. It includes behavior having a positive and social content as implied by "directing a group." It does not include behavior serving only the individual goal attainment.

In the earlier studies referred to above, in which persons in "leadership positions" were asked to describe *what* they do in carrying out their jobs, some indication of the different sorts of things that individuals in leadership positions do was obtained. By comparing percentage of time spent on specific items such as planning, supervision, working with other persons (in contrast with individual effort) as reported by individuals at different levels in the group, a tentative criterion was established for indicating *what* individuals in the top "leadership" positions do. This criterion likewise provides a basis for singling out what may constitute leader behavior in a specific group.

This definition left unspecified the *hows* of the directing, except that it be toward a shared goal. It does set some general boundaries to the part of the total behavior of an individual which members of the staff desired to describe as leader behavior.

During the process of evaluating the over-all research program attendant to attempts to work in the *how* of leader behavior, the question of areas, classifications, or dimensions for the description of leader behavior was raised. Among the problems discussed were (1) relative independence of areas or dimensions, (2) meaning with reference to theoretical systems or bodies of knowledge common to psychology, sociology, or social science in general, (3) level of analysis, i.e., whether behavior is to be described in large, molar units or divided into molecular elements, and (4) possibility of objective measurement and inference from the frequency or amount of the behavior in question.

A classification of areas or dimensions of leader behavior entirely satisfactory to any one member of the staff was found to be extremely difficult to attain. As representatives of separate disciplines, each with its own orientation or problem approach (not to mention individual preferences or inclinations), the staff members found considerable difficulty in reaching agreement even at the verbal level on what was proposed as a common instrument. However, after extended discussions, a list of dimensions was tentatively designated. Staff members maintained reservations concerning the independence of the dimensions, meaning with reference to theoretical systems, and the possibility of objective measurement of the dimensions. Many questions about possible descriptive categories of leader behavior were postponed. The tentatively designated dimensions of leader behavior were:

1. Integration—acts which tend to increase cooperation among members or decrease competition among them.
2. Communication—acts which increase the understanding of and knowledge about what is going on in the group.

DEVELOPMENT OF DESCRIPTIONS

3. Production emphasis—acts which are oriented toward volume of work accomplished.
4. Representation—acts which speak for the group in interaction with outside agencies.
5. Fraternization—acts which tend to make the leader a part of the group.
6. Organization—acts which lead to differentiation of duties and which prescribe ways of doing things.
7. Evaluation—acts which have to do with distribution of rewards (or punishment).
8. Initiation—acts which lead to change in group activities.
9. Domination—acts which disregard the ideas or person of members of the group.

These nine areas provided a framework for the collection of specific items of leader behavior which were later closely examined and evaluated.

ITEM CONSTRUCTION

Each member of the staff of the Personnel Research Board wrote items of behavior which seemed to apply to the above areas. Suggestions for items were drawn from personal experiences, and from familiarity with the literature concerned with leadership. To increase the range of behavior comprehended by the items, beyond that suggested by the relatively homogenous experience of the members of the staff, a method of obtaining items from a larger population was devised. Members of two advanced university classes wrote 48 items each—12 items in each of 4 different areas—as an exercise in item construction. The instructions to these students emphasized the following points:

1. Items should describe specific behavior, *not* general traits or characteristics.
2. Items should apply to various kinds of organizational structures, groups or situations. They should not be so specific as to apply to only a few groups or situations.
3. Items should be worded in terms meaningful to the respondents.
4. An item should apply specifically to the variable for which it is written. It may also overlap other dimensions of behavior.
5. The items should be written in the present tense.
6. The items should begin with the pronoun "He."

7. The item should be limited to one unit of behavior (should not be "double barreled").
8. The items should not contain adverbs referring to the frequency with which the behavior occurs (always, never, etc.).
9. The items should not be emotionally or evaluatively toned except as that tone is an inseparable part of the behavior it describes.

After minor editing, 1,790 items remained from all sources. From these items, 150 were to be selected and arranged in the form of a preliminary questionnaire.

ITEM SELECTION FOR A PRELIMINARY QUESTIONNAIRE

The first step in the selection of specific items from the large collection of 1,790, was an attempt to classify them into the 9 areas mentioned above. Although written to belong to specific areas, it was soon discovered that many items overlapped several areas, or seemed to belong in a different area from that for which they were intended.

One of the 9 dimensions was assigned to each member of the research staff who examined each of the 1,790 items to determine whether or not it belonged to his assigned dimension. By compiling the results of this examination, it was possible to list items which appeared to belong to one dimension only, or to two, three, or even four dimensions. These lists were supplied to each member of the staff, and served as the basis for group discussion of each item. In these discussions, items were considered for overlap of content, relative freedom from overlap with items in other dimensions, range of content, general evaluation tone, etc. Minor editing of some items plus the writing of a few additional items believed to cover omissions or gaps in content were also accomplished during these group discussions.

Approximately 200 items survived this selection procedure. The staff then decided to reduce the number to 150 items to be suitable for use with IBM Test Answer Sheets. It was also decided to subclassify items within dimensions in order to examine more systematically the content emphasized. During this second screening, the dimensions were redefined to correspond more closely with the actual content of items in the category. The redefined dimensions are listed below, together with the number of items retained in each subcategory of the dimension.

Initiation—The dimension, initiation, is described by the frequency with which a leader originates, facilitates, or resists new ideas and new practices. The subcategories are:
1. Origination of new ideas or practices—7 items.
2. Facilitation of new ideas or practices—4 items.
3. Resistance to new ideas or practices—4 items.

Membership—The dimension, membership, is described by the frequency which a leader mixes with the group, stresses informal interaction between himself and members, or interchanges personal services with members. The subcategories are:
1. Mixing with members—4 items.
2. Informal interaction—5 items.
3. Interchanging personal services—6 items.

Representation—The dimension, representation, is described by the frequency with which a leader defends his group against attack, advances the interests of his group and acts in behalf of his group. The subcategories are:
1. Defends against attack—5 items.
2. Advances the interests of the group—7 items.
3. Acts in behalf of the group—4 items.

Integration—The dimension, integration, is described by the frequency which a leader subordinates individual behavior, encourages pleasant group atmosphere, reduces conflicts between members, or promotes individual adjustment to the group. The subcategories are:
1. Subordination of individual behavior—6 items.
2. Encouraging pleasant group atmosphere—4 items.
3. Reducing conflicts between members—5 items.
4. Promoting individual adjustment to the group—2 items.

Organization—The dimension, organization, is described by the frequency with which a leader defines or structures his own work, the work of other members, or the relationships among members in the performance of their work. The subcategories are:

1. Definition or structuring of own work—4 items.
2. Definition or structuring of work of other members—9 items.
3. Definition or structuring of relationships among members in performance of their work—5 items.

Domination—The dimension, domination, is described by the frequency with which the leader restricts the behavior of individuals or the group in action, decision-making, or expression of opinion. The subcategories are:

1. Restriction of action—6 items.
2. Restriction of decision-making—8 items.
3. Restriction of expression of opinion—5 items.

Communication—The dimension, communication, is described by the frequency with which a leader provides information to members, seeks information from them, facilitates exchange of information, or shows awareness of affairs pertaining to the group. The subcategories are:

1. Informing members—8 items.
2. Seeking information—4 items.
3. Facilitating exchange of information—4 items.
4. Being aware of affairs pertaining to the group—6 items.

Recognition—The dimension, recognition, is described by the frequency with which a leader engages in behavior which expresses approval or disapproval of the behavior of group members. The subcategories are:

1. Acts expressing approval—7 items.
2. Acts expressing disapproval—7 items.

Production—The dimension, production, is described by the frequency with which a leader sets levels of effort or achievement, or prods members for greater effort or achievement. The subcategories are:

1. Setting levels of achievement or effort—6 items.
2. Prodding members for effort or achievement—6 items.

The Communication dimension was split into Communication Up and Communication Down in the construction of the questionnaire, making a total of 10 dimensions.

THE PRELIMINARY QUESTIONNAIRE

When the 150 items of leader behavior had been selected and classified by area or dimension, they were arranged to form the Leader Behavior Description Questionnaire. Items were randomized and the 10 dimensions to which they applied dropped out of the picture so far as the respondent was concerned.

At this point, a decision had to be made regarding the format. The purpose, as has been stated, was to obtain from respondents objective descriptions of leader behavior. In the use of items selected, however, the staff anticipated that the *value tone* associated with leader behavior would contribute to an intermingling of the *quality* of leadership with objective observation of the leader's actual behavior.

A "forced choice" format was considered as one method of meeting the problem of evaluation tone in the items. This technique assumes that where two items having similar evaluation tone are paired so as to force the respondent to choose between them, this decision will be based on other considerations than the evaluation tone of the item. It might be expected that descriptions so obtained would correspond rather closely to objective observation of behavior.

Two objections were raised to the "forced choice" format, which subsequently led to its rejection in the preliminary questionnaire. First, in order to construct a "forced choice" questionnaire, it would be necessary to know the relative value tone of each item as viewed by a representative respondent. This would have involved a pre-preliminary administration of the items to secure data from which to determine each item's relative evaluative tone. The second objection stemmed from a desire to obtain quantitatively comparable statements of the frequency with which a "leader" engages in an item of behavior. This would be impossible with a "forced choice" format, where frequency of occurence of an item of behavior would have to be eliminated along with the elimination of value tone. The relation between value tone and frequency of occurence of a specific behavior will be apparent in the following example:

1. He always keeps the group informed (high value tone).
2. He never keeps the group informed (low value tone).

It would not be possible to measure frequency of acts of behavior and at the same time eliminate value considerations.

In the light of these difficulties the staff decided to use a multiple choice format for the questionnaire. Five choices were presented in conjunction with each item. These choices were adverbs expressing frequency of the behavior stated by the item. For example, the first item in the questionnaire was as follows:

1. He plans his day's activities in detail.
    A. Always   *B.* Often   *C.* Occasionally   *D.* Seldom   *E.* Never

The choice of the adverbs to follow each item was a problem given special consideration. By use of these adverbs it was hoped that two things might be accomplished: (1) To divide the range of frequency of behavior into approximately equal psychological steps by the five choices, and (2) To coordinate the adverbs with the item in such a way that there would be no obvious reason to choose one response rather than the other, so far as the instrument itself would be concerned. Care was taken, for that reason, to avoid awkward language in the transition between item and answer choices.

A list of 42 adverbs expressing *frequency* and/or extent of engaging in behavior described by an item was obtained by compiling suggestions from staff members. This list was then presented to each staff member who served as a judge in a paired-comparison evaluation of each adverb against every other adverb on the list, using as a criterion the extent to which it expressed frequency or extent of occurrence.

Three combinations of five frequency adverbs were selected from the list to be used as multiple choice responses to the items of leader behavior. The three combinations and their modal values are listed below:

Combination A		Combination B		Combination C	
Response Alternative	Mode	Response Alternative	Mode	Response Alternative	Mode
Always	41	Often	32	A great deal	38
Often	32	Fairly often	27	Fairly much	26
Occasionally	21	Occasionally	21	To some degree	21
Seldom	11	Once in awhile	13	Comparatively	13
Never	0	Very seldom	8	Not at all	1

Combinations *A* and *B* are composed of adverbs expressing frequency; combination *C* contains adverbs expressing extent. *A* differs from *B* in that extreme frequencies have been omitted and the resulting narrower range of frequency is spread among the five steps.

Members of the staff considered each item to be included in the questionnaire to determine which one of the three response combinations would most likely meet the two criteria mentioned above for the choice of adverbs to follow an item. Wherever possible, combination *A* was favored over the other two combinations. A list of the items in the Leader Behavior Description Questionnaire is shown in Appendix A.

PLAN FOR TESTING QUESTIONNAIRE

A point was reached in the development of the instrument when it became apparent that a number of remaining questions could only be answered on the basis of experience, i.e., through administering the items to a large sample of respondents. These questions involved both the dimensional classification of the items and the performance of each item itself.

Among the questions relating to the classification system were the following:

1. What is the reliability of the dimension scores for each area?
2. To what extent do the areas of classification overlap?
3. What is the relation between each dimension score and the over-all evaluation of a leader?
4. How do descriptions given by subordinates compare with descriptions given by leaders themselves on each dimension score?

With respect to the individual items contrasted with the classification areas, the following questions were raised:

1. What is the distribution of responses to each item?
2. How are the responses to each item related to general, over-all evaluation of the leader?
3. How is each item related to each dimensional classification score?
4. Is there a difference when an item is used to describe a leader superior to the respondent, or when it is used by the respondent to describe himself?

To secure data from which tentative answers to these questions might be obtained, the Leader Behavior Description Questionnaire (hereafter designated as LBDQ) was administered to 357 individuals. Of these respondents, 205 described a leader of a group in which they were members or had recently been members, while 152 described themselves as leaders. In addition to completing the LBDQ, each respondent completed the following forms:

1. Evaluation of the leader's behavior generally
2. Evaluation of 10 specific areas of the leader's behavior
3. A short questionnaire on the reverse side of an answer sheet concerning information about the group, the group's leaders, and about the respondent himself. The respondent was not required to identify himself or the leader he described but could elect to use a code identifying the separate forms he completed.

An attempt was made to select as catholic a sample of groups and leaders as could be obtained in a summer school college population. The sample included several high school teachers and administrators as well as the traditional sophomore.

Twenty-nine different types of groups and group situations could be identified among the 357 completed questionnaires, ranging from informal social groups to military organizations. As might be expected, groups with school and college associations predominated, although other occupationally oriented and religious groups were included. A majority (205) described the leader's behavior as observed by a member, although 152 described themselves as leaders.

A breakdown of the biographical information likewise revealed a reasonably catholic sample of respondents. Ages ranged from 18 to 55, with a modal grouping of 102 in the 24-29 class. The 310 male respondents far outnumbered the female. Again as was to be expected, educational level of the respondents was high, the majority falling in the range from college sophomore to at least one year of graduate work completed. In terms of the group situation described, the largest number had been associated with the organization from one to two years, although the upper range of this variable was 14 years.

ANALYSIS OF ITEMS COMPOSING THE LEADER BEHAVIOR DESCRIPTION QUESTIONNAIRE

Four kinds of information were desired concerning the performance of each of the 150 items in the leader behavior description questionnaire.

1. How are respondents' descriptions of their leader distributed among the 5 choices of adverbs presented to them?

2. To what extent did the over-all evaluation of the leader's ability affect the separate items? Is the respondent's evaluation of the particular leader's leadership quality associated in any consistent way with the choice of words to describe his behavior?

3. Are the items which make up a dimension internally consistent? Are they measuring the same thing? To what extent might an item assigned to one category perform more consistently as a measure of another category?

4. With respect to the above three types of information, does the instrument perform differently when used for self-description than when used to describe someone else?

To secure information about these four types of problems, a complete item analysis was made of the descriptions given by subordinates of their leaders, and by leaders of themselves. An IBM Test Scoring Machine was utilized to secure counts of the number of individuals describing a leader by each of the five adverbs following the items.

For an item to be most useful, all responses should be sufficiently attractive to be used in the description of at least some of the leaders. No single response should be used so frequently as to exclude the other possible responses. The responses which were seldom used were the more extreme frequency responses, i.e., *always, a great deal,* or *never.* The extreme responses, *always* and *never,* were less frequently used by leaders in describing themselves than by subordinates in describing leaders.

Leaders, in describing their own behavior (as compared with subordinates describing their leaders' behavior), tended more frequently to use responses to an item which were favorable in tone.

Also, while self-description responses to certain items tended to concentrate toward either a higher or lower frequency level (when contrasted with subordinate descriptions) these items were not equally distributed among the dimension categories.

Greatest concentration at the higher or lower frequency levels occurred in the Communications dimensions. Integration and Recognition were fairly close seconds. Production, Representation, Initiation, and Organization showed the least tendency to be influenced by the type of description being considered. Can it be that leaders are less able to appraise their behavior with respect to communicative acts than they are in other areas of behavior?

THE RELATION BETWEEN LEADER BEHAVIOR ITEMS AND GENERAL EVALUATION OF LEADERS

One of the principal goals in attempting to develop a questionnaire for the description of leader behavior is to obtain descriptions that are objective. A rating scale, on the other hand, is used to evaluate rather than to describe behavior. In order to determine whether the descriptions were being made on an objective basis, each respondent was asked not only to describe the behavior of his leader, but also to evaluate his quality as a leader. The evaluation was made on a separate scale for rating general leadership quality. The rating scale consisted of 7 steps ranging from "Perfect" to "Poor." Leaders who described their own behavior on the LBDQ also evaluated their own leadership by checking the appropriate response on the rating scale.

In examining the relations between leader behavior dimension scores and over-all evaluation of the leader's leadership quality, a substantial lack of independence was noted. This lack of independence between descriptions and evaluations is probably related to the difficulty of making statements about the frequency with which a leader engages in a significant item of behavior without, at the same time, evaluating his behavior. However, *it may be possible* to find items of behavior which have variance in common with a dimension of leader behavior but which do not correlate with general evaluations of leaders. If such items could be found one would feel more confident that in using them, a description of a leader's behavior would be obtained that was not greatly influenced by general "halo" factors based on the leader's general reputation, personal friendship, etc.

In order to determine the relationship between the response made to an item and general over-all evaluation of the leader described, tetrachoric correlation coefficients were computed. The correlations are shown in Appendix B. The 5 possible responses to each item were dichotomized at a point where, as nearly as possible, 50 per cent of the responses were in each of two categories. The evaluation ratings were also dichotomized on the same 50–50 basis. The correlation between item scores and over-all evaluation ratings, when both descriptions and evaluation are made by the same subordinate, is quite high for most items. The range for tetrachoric coefficients was found to be from —.53 to .75. Negative coefficients occur most frequently for items expressing Domination behavior. Of the 150 coefficients for description made by subordinates, 34 were .50 or over in absolute magnitude, while 90 were more than +.30 in magnitude.

When the leader describes his own behavior and evaluates his own leadership quality, the coefficients expressing the relation between item responses and over-all evaluation ratings were not so large as in the case of subordinate descriptions. The range of these self-description tetrachoric correlation coefficients is from —.31 to .52. Only one coefficient was larger than +.50 while 132 were less than +.30. Leaders, when describing their own behavior, as compared with subordinates when describing the behavior of their leaders, tend to respond to the items in a manner less dependent upon their ratings of the quality of their leadership.

The considerable number of large differences (33 over .40) between corresponding pairs of correlation coefficients make it clear that leaders tend to value or to describe their own behavior differently than subordinates describe and evaluate the behavior of leaders. One would, therefore, not expect self-descriptions of leader behavior to be capable of substitution for descriptions made by subordinates. Is there a major difference between the kinds of behavior "leaders" considered "good" as compared with the kinds of behavior valued by subordinates? On the other hand, it may be asked whether leaders who see their own behavior as good leadership are individuals who tend to describe their own behavior in a way that differs from the way subordinates would describe "good" leadership behavior? These questions are not answered by the present investigation. Here, we may only conclude that there are likely to be major differences between leaders' self-description of their behavior and descriptions of leader behavior by subordinates.

INTERNAL CONSISTENCY ITEM ANALYSIS

One of the central problems in developing a measuring instrument to express degree of specific dimensions of behavior is that of obtaining items which sample an area or dimension of behavior, and items which, when combined, yield a reliable total score. For an item to contribute to a reliable (composite) total score it must sample the same kinds of behavior as do the other items which go to make up the total score. An item which meets this requirement will show variations in the responses made to it which are concomitant with variations in the total score. The extent of this concomitant variation is expressed by the correlation between the responses to the item and the total dimension score.

As already noted, some reservations were felt concerning the assignment of items to dimension categories under the assumption that these categories were independent. In view of these reservations, it was decided to extend the usual internal-consistency item-analysis procedure of correlating each item within an area with the total score for the area or dimension to which the item was assigned. Correlations were not only computed between an item and its own dimension total score, but with each of the 9 other dimension total scores to which it had *not* been assigned. It was anticipated that this procedure would yield information which would be valuable for two purposes: (1) items which failed to correlate highly with their total dimension scores could be eliminated; (2) items which have variance in common with dimensions other than that to which they were assigned could be removed with the expectation of increasing the independence of the dimension total scores.

Tetrachoric correlation coefficients were computed to express the relationship between the responses to each item of leader behavior, dichotomized at as near a 50–50 division as possible, and each total dimension score dichotomized at each median score. Coefficients were obtained for a sample of 200 descriptions made by subordinates, and 150 descriptions made by leaders of their own behavior. Correlation coefficients are reported in such a manner that a high frequency response to the items *as stated* in the questionnaire, when associated with a high dimension total score, results in a positive value.

It may be seen in Appendix B that relatively few of the items satisfy the criterion of a high correlation with own dimension and a low correlation with all other dimensions, particularly when both self-descriptions and descriptions by subordinates are considered. A larger proportion of the items meets this criterion when the items are used by leaders to describe themselves than when used by subordinates to describe their leaders. Approximately half of the items are more highly correlated with one or more other dimensions than with their own dimension. It appears, therefore, that the assignment of items to the hypothesized dimension categories fails to meet the requirement of independence between dimensions.

The question as to whether the assignment of items to dimensions by members of the staff was any better than random assignment is raised. In considering this question, it must be recognized that part of the correlation between an item and the dimension score to which it was assigned may be due to the spurious factor of the item variance being part of the total score variance. It is difficult to determine for any given item how much of the total dimension variance is contributed by that item. If it is assumed that each item makes an equal contribution to its total dimension score, and that there are 15 items for each dimension (actually the number of items per dimension ranges from 10 for Communication to 20 for Domination), an approximate average correction may be computed which could be applied to these assumed spurious correlations. This spurious correlation factor would be approximately .26. In view of this consideration, in conjunction with "uncorrected" data, one must entertain considerable doubt about the dimensionality of the 10 leader behavior "dimensions."

DISTRIBUTION OF DIMENSION SCORES AND ESTIMATES OF RELIABILITY

Although the item analysis has been discussed first, the actual scoring of the returned questionnaires was done on a dimensional basis. Scoring keys were constructed for each of the 10 dimensions.

The distributions of scores for the dimensions, where the descriptions were made by subordinates, indicate considerable range of scores, but with a skewedness toward behavior regarded as socially most acceptable. For example, the descriptions tend in the direction of less frequent domination, more frequent initiation, membership, representation, integration, etc. The scores for self-descriptions of leaders show, on the average, less range of variability and perhaps even more of a tendency to concentrate at the more highly valued end of each dimension continuum.

Reliability of the dimension scores, where descriptions were made by subordinates, was considered sufficiently high for purposes of establishing "high" and "low" categories for item analysis. The reliabilities of self-description dimension scores are consistently lower than where description was made by subordinates. Odd-even reliability coefficients for the dimension scores are shown in Tables 1 and 2.

TABLE 1—Description of 205 Leaders by Subordinates: Intercorrelation Between Dimension Scores and Their Correlation with Other Variables, Reliabilities, Means, and Standard Deviations

Dimensions and Variables	Leadership Dimensions									
	1	2	3	4	5	6	7	8	9	10
	r	r	r	r	r	r	r	r	r	r
Dimensions										
1 Domination		—.56	—.64	—.46	—.57	—.10	—.50	—.55	—.53	.35
2 Initiation	—.56		.51	.60	.60	.37	.57	.63	.59	.14
3 Membership	—.64	.51		.58	.65	.24	.60	.62	.62	—.12
4 Representation	—.46	.60	.58		.77	.58	.69	.77	.72	.22
5 Integration	—.57	.60	.65	.77		.56	.75	.81	.75	.12
6 Organization	—.10	.37	.24	.58	.56		.65	.65	.57	.50
7 Communication Up	—.50	.57	.60	.69	.75	.65		.79	.74	.16
8 Communication Down	—.55	.63	.62	.77	.81	.65	.79		.78	.21
9 Recognition	—.53	.59	.62	.72	.75	.57	.74	.78		.11
10 Production	.35	.14	—.12	.22	.12	.50	.16	.21	.11	
Adequacy Ratings										
11 General Adequacy	—.42	.60	.48	.59	.66	.51	.62	.67	.62	.11
12 Specific Adequacy	.44	.33	.38	.46	.38	.48	.52	.22	.28	—.44
Biographical Data										
13 Number of Members	—.07	.12	.04	.23	.19	.22	.18	.21	.17	.24
14 Time Together	.38	—.27	—.18	—.10	—.19	—.03	—.16	—.18	—.14	.06
15 Leader's Age	.21	.01	—.27	—.16	—.13	.03	—.07	—.09	—.09	.10
16 Leader's Sex	—.13	.12	.11	.10	.15	.09	.10	.13	.10	.12
17 Length of Leadership	.06	.00	—.03	—.14	—.06	—.05	—.03	—.03	.01	.02
18 Respondent's Age	.10	.01	—.23	—.04	—.09	—.05	—.11	—.11	—.14	—.04
19 Respondent's Time in Group	—.10	.07	.12	.05	.05	.00	.03	.05	.10	.05
Reliability										
Odd-Even Reliability	.88	.85	.81	.88	.80	.87	.87	.84	.71	.78
Mean	4.4	5.9	6.9	9.5	9.2	12.1	9.9	12.0	4.0	3.0
Standard Deviation	12.7	8.8	9.3	9.7	9.0	9.6	5.8	7.7	6.8	6.9

$r = .18$ is significant at the .01 level.

TABLE 2—Self-Descriptions of 152 Leaders: Intercorrelations Between Dimension Scores and Their Correlation with Other Variables, Reliabilities, Means, and Standard Deviations

Dimensions and Variables	Leadership Dimensions									
	1	2	3	4	5	6	7	8	9	10
	r	r	r	r	r	r	r	r	r	r
Dimensions										
1 Domination		—.24	—.40	—.06	—.19	.29	—.27	—.17	—.04	.28
2 Initiation	—.24		.34	.50	.45	.27	.33	.45	.28	.21
3 Membership	—.40	.34		.30	.44	.01	.37	.37	.15	.08
4 Representation	—.06	.50	.30		.58	.57	.44	.60	.43	.34
5 Integration	—.19	.45	.44	.58		.38	.46	.59	.33	.27
6 Organization	.29	.27	.01	.57	.38		.38	.54	.38	.50
7 Communication Up	—.27	.33	.37	.44	.46	.38		.61	.36	.15
8 Communication Down	—.17	.45	.37	.60	.59	.54	.61		.43	.38
9 Recognition	—.04	.28	.15	.43	.33	.38	.36	.43		.34
10 Production	.28	.21	.08	.34	.27	.50	.15	.38	.34	
Adequacy Ratings										
11 General Adequacy	.12	.22	.13	.31	.34	.34	.13	.34	.10	.21
12 Specific Adequacy	.23	.13	—.05	.30	.26	.15	.08	.17	.15	—.24
Biographical Data										
13 Number of Members	—.05	—.09	—.15	.09	.03	.04	—.07	.03	—.03	.13
14 Time Together	.34	—.12	—.19	.01	—.15	.16	.03	—.15	—.10	—.05
15 Leader's Age	—.15	.26	.11	.17	.21	—.03	.01	.11	.17	.03
16 Leader's Sex	—.17	—.01	.12	.03	.02	—.09	.09	.06	.01	.01
17 Length of Leadership	.02	.06	—.06	.09	.12	—.03	—.11	.08	.10	.15
18 Length of Membership	.01	—.02	—.03	—.06	.00	—.14	—.14	.00	—.01	.11
Reliability										
Odd-Even Reliability	.76	.54	.58	.82	.58	.84	.64	.66	.59	.75
Mean	12.0	9.6	12.8	13.0	15.3	16.8	14.0	17.2	7.9	3.4
Standard Deviation	9.0	5.5	6.6	6.9	6.0	7.9	3.4	4.9	4.5	5.3

$r = .21$ is significant at the .01 level.

INTERCORRELATION BETWEEN DIMENSION SCORES

One of the principal questions it was hoped might be answered by an analysis of the empirical data was the extent to which the total dimension scores measure independent areas. The intercorrelations are shown in Tables 1 and 2. The intercorrelations tend to reinforce the anticipation that the leader behavior dimensions were not independent. Most of the dimensions show substantial overlap with one another. In many cases the degree of correlation between dimensions was approximately as great as the reliabilities of the measures would permit. The intercorrelations among dimension scores for description made by subordinates were consistently higher than those based on self-description. This, also, may be due to the relative restriction of variability in the self-description score rather than an actual difference in the degree of overlap among the basic dimension categories. The Production dimension is most independent of other dimensions in descriptions by subordinates.

FACTOR ANALYSIS OF THE INTERCORRELATION OF DIMENSION SCORES

In order to explore the structure of the interrelations among the descriptive dimensions, a factor analysis was made of the intercorrelations shown in Tables 1 and 2. The general, over-all evaluation rating of leadership quality was also included in each matrix in order to estimate the degree to which lack of independence may be due to evaluation "halo." Two factor analyses were made; one for the matrix of intercorrelation for subordinates' descriptions of their leaders, and a second for leaders' descriptions of their own behavior. The matrices were factored following Thurstone's centroid method. The centroid factor loadings of the three factors which were extracted are presented in Tables 3 and 4.

TABLE 3—Centroid Factor Loadings of Leader Behavior Description Dimensions—Descriptions Made by Subordinates

Dimension	Centroid Factor			
	I	II	III	h^2
Domination (Non)	.579	.622	.193	.759
Initiation	.727	.187	—.313	.661
Membership	.686	.381	.148	.638
Representation	.847	—.051	—.029	.721
Integration	.884	.073	.076	.793
Organization	.675	—.553	.102	.772
Communication Up	.860	—.055	.194	.780
Communication Down	.914	—.044	.106	.850
Recognition	.854	.051	.106	.743
Production	.201	—.655	—.249	.531
Evaluation	.746	.062	—.112	.572

Rotation of axes to obtain most meaningful structure presented two problems. First, oblique solutions were rejected because such solutions would not be consistent with the basic requirement of a system of independent dimensions. Second, it appeared quite obvious on inspection of the centroid loadings that with the possible exception of Production, each dimension contained a sizable variance in common with the evaluation ratings. It was decided that simplest

TABLE 4—Centroid Factor Loadings of Leader Behavior Description Dimensions—Descriptions Made by the Leader of Himself

Dimension	Centroid Factor			
	I	II	III	h²
Domination (Non)	.174	.664	.079	.477
Initiation	.612	—.142	—.142	.415
Membership	.489	—.469	—.133	.477
Representation	.763	.139	—.055	.601
Integration	.745	—.095	—.182	.597
Organization	.589	.581	.109	.696
Communication Up	.663	—.161	.326	.572
Communication Down	.821	.050	.214	.722
Recognition	.528	.149	.155	.325
Production	.436	.484	—.176	.455
Evaluation	.378	.215	.071	.194

structure might be sacrificed to the objective of obtaining as clear meaning as possible of three orthogonal principal dimensions. The factors were defined on the basis of the rotated factor loadings.

Factor I was tentatively designated as *Maintenance of Membership Character*. The rotated dimension loadings on this factor are listed below:

Dimension	Subordinates	Self
1. Domination (Non)	.86	.58
2. Membership	.78	.69
3. Integration	.75	.58
4. Initiation	.71	.52
5. Recognition	.71	.18
6. Communication Down	.69	.42
7. Communication Up	.64	.45
8. Representation	.64	.39
9. Evaluation	.64	.06

This factor represents behavior of a leader which permits him to be considered a "good fellow" by his subordinates. It reflects behavior which is socially agreeable to group numbers. Factor I carries a high degree of the evaluation rating variance for subordinates' descriptions but not so for self description. However, the loadings on the dimensions make it possible to identify this factor as one related to behavior that increases a leader's acceptability as a group member. It seems consistent that this behavior is more highly related to general leadership evaluation on the part of group members subordinate to a leader than on the part of the leader himself. Recognition also shows a marked difference in loading when the two types of description are compared. It seems that behavior which is concerned with a leader taking cognizance of a member's contribution to his group is viewed differently by the leader and subordinate. This will be discussed further in connection with the second factor.

Factor II was identified as *Objective Attainment Behavior.* Dimensions having highest loadings on this factor are listed below:

Dimension	Subordinates	Self
1. Production	.66	.67
2. Organization	.57	.77
3. Representation	.43	.64
4. Initiation	.41	.37
5. Communication Down	.36	.55
6. Integration	.30	.50
7. Recognition	.28	.43
8. Evaluation	.37	.39

This factor has to do with behavior related to the output of the group. The appearance of both Initiation and Organization among the high loading on this factor, at first, appeared incongruous. It will be recalled that Initiation contains an element of origination and readiness for change, while Organization stresses definition and structuring. These may be viewed as two opposing kinds of behavior. However, a second element of Initiation involves taking positive action in establishing goals or objectives which may well fit into the same factor with that part of Organization behavior which has to do with structuring group activities in a way that members may work toward an objective. Representation fits into the factor to the degree the leader behavior is a vehicle of group accomplishment in relation to outside groups, agencies, forces, etc. The difference between descriptions made by subordinates and those made by leaders of their own behavior are very striking on this factor. Leaders take a more comprehensive view of the objectives of group activities. They emphasize organization and activities of a human relation nature, along with the more tangible products of the group as part of objective attainment. This interpretation would be consistent with the appearance of substantial loadings of the dimensions Communication Down, Integration, and Recognition on this factor only in the case of leader's self description.

Factor III was identified as *Group Interaction Facilitation Behavior*. Dimensions having highest loadings on this factor are listed below:

Dimension	Subordinates	Self
1. Organization	.65	.30
2. Communication Up	.56	.55
3. Communication Down	.51	.49
4. Recognition	.43	.33
5. Integration	.38	.10

This factor has highest loading on dimensions involving behavior which would enable group members to recognize their functions in the group, and to know what is going on. The factor might be called "structuring communication." However, in view of the minor loading on Recognition and Integration, the broader interpretation as "interaction facilitation" is more appropriate. The major difference between the description made by subordinates and leader's description of their own behavior, with respect to this factor, is smaller loadings on the dimension Organization and Integration. These differences also fit into the general interpretation of the differences between leaders and followers as they view the functions of leader behavior. Followers view Organization and Integration behavior as part of facilitation of group interaction. The leaders view the same behavior as more of a part of objective attainment.

In summary, the factor analysis identifies, within the intercorrelations among the 10 dimensions, three general factors. The first is general social agreeableness, highly related to evaluation ratings. The second is a drive for objective or goal attainment. The third stresses the mechanics of effective interaction of group members. With some minor differences in loadings on certain dimensions these three factors are common to both types of description.

RELATIONS BETWEEN LEADER BEHAVIOR DIMENSIONS AND BIOGRAPHICAL DATA VARIABLES

As was indicated above, certain items of biographical data were collected about the group which the leader led, about the leader, and about the respondent describing the leader. Information obtained from the following questions was correlated with each of the Leader Behavior Description dimension scores:

Information about the group
  Number of members in the group..............................
  Amount of time the group spent together..............................
Information about the group leader
  Leader's approximate age..............................
  Leader's sex..............................
  How long he has been leader of the group..............................
Information about the respondent
  Age..............................
  Length of time he has been a member of the group..............................

Most of the correlations shown in Tables 1 and 2 between leader behavior descriptions and biographical items are low. The number of members (size of group) is related to a statistically significant but small degree to the leader behavior dimensions Representation, Integration, Organization, Communication, and Production as described by subordinates. In the larger groups, subordinates report their leaders as more frequently engaging in the behavior expressed by these dimensions. The length of time the group spends together is significantly associated with the Domination behavior reported for the leaders, and negatively related to reported Initiation, Membership, Integration, and Communication Down. These relationships suggest a number of interpretations, a few of which are listed below:

1. Leaders in the group whose members spend much time together tend to become "bosses" rather than "leaders" in the sense of "suggesters" or "facilitators" of group activities.

2. Groups which spend much time together are those in which a leader takes a dominant but non-initiating role.

3. Membership in a group where members spend much time together produces a sensitivity in members to behavior of their leader which can be interpreted as dominative.

The three remaining significant correlations involve the leaders' and respondents' ages. Older leaders are seen to display more Domination behavior. Older members tend to report leaders showing less Membership behavior and members tend to describe older leaders with low Membership scores. These tendencies raise questions as to the function of age in the problems of leadership.

Leaders of groups which spend much time together report that they engage in domination behavior more frequently than do leaders of groups which spend less time together. This agrees with the reports of subordinates.

Older leaders report engaging in Initiation and Integration behavior more frequently than younger leaders. Do older leaders have a somewhat different perception of their roles than do younger leaders?

RELATIONS BETWEEN LEADER BEHAVIOR DESCRIPTION DIMENSIONS AND EVALUATION OF LEADERSHIP QUALITY

Two measures of leadership quality were obtained from each respondent. The first was a general over-all rating of leadership quality on a seven-point scale ranging from "Perfect" to "Poor." The second was a specific rating on each of the 10 leader behavior dimensions in terms of "Too much" or "Too little." For example, a respondent indicated the correspondence of his judgment of the leader's actual frequency of domination with his idea of what would be the right amount by checking on the following scale.

1. The extent to which he dominates his group as a leader:

Too much	A little too much	About right	Not quite enough	Too little

Thus, there was available, not only a description of leader behavior for each of the dimensions, but also a separate measure of the respondent's satisfaction or dissatisfaction with the dimension of behavior described. In scoring these specific rating scales, a score of 5 was given to the response, "Too much," and a score of 1 to the response, "Too little." It will be noted that this system of scoring differs from that employed for the single scale for evaluating general leadership quality. In the latter, a high score indicated "good" leadership. In the 10 scales for evaluating the 10 specific dimensions of behavior, a "poor" performance with respect to a dimension might be expressed by either "Too much" or "Too little." If the items were scored to stress quality of performance, one would assign a value of 1 to "Too much" and "Too little," a value of 2 to "A little too much" and "Not quite enough," and the highest value of 3 to "About right." However, the objective of securing evaluative ratings for each of the dimensions was to obtain some verification of dimension total scores as objective measures of the different dimensions. This consideration would argue against putting "Too much" and "Too little" ratings together in the same scoring category. A second difficulty is encountered in attempting to obtain a meaningful score from the ratings. "About right" is likely to be a degree of the dimension, shifting from situation to situation, and bearing no constant relation to any actual frequency of dominating behavior. The 1 to 5 scoring system is defensible only to the degree that the meaning of "About right" remains constant from situation to situation.

Each of the leader behavior description dimensions, with the exception of Production, showed a definite relation to the general evaluation given a leader by a subordinate (Table 1). The dimensions Domination, Membership, Communication Up, and Recognition were not significantly related to general over-all leadership quality evaluation when the leaders described themselves and evaluated their own leadership quality (Table 2). It is also found that the correlations between dimension scores and over-all evaluation are, on the average, larger for the description made by subordinates than for the descriptions made by the leaders themselves (Tables I and 2). This again may be simply a reflection of less variability among the self-description scores.

The comparison between self-description and description by others is of special interest in the case of the dimension Domination. Leaders who evaluate themselves highly tend (although not significantly) to report themselves as more frequently engaging in Domination behavior. On the other hand, subordinates see Domination behavior and poor leadership quality as going together. Perhaps it is in the area of interpretation of what behavior is dominant that leaders tend to be least perceptive of group member's reactions to their behavior.

Significant correlations are found between descriptions of leader behavior and specific evaluations of the same behavior for each of the 10 dimensions, when subordinates do the describing and the rating. Where leaders describe themselves and make the evaluations of their own behavior, significant correlations are found for the dimensions Domination, Representation, Integration, and Production.

Of special interest was the finding that specific evaluative ratings of Production were *negatively* related to descriptions of Production behavior. This was true both for the self-descriptions and the descriptions made by subordinates. It appears that leaders who are described as more frequently engaging in Production behavior are also evaluated as engaging in *"too little"* Production. Is it that those situations which stimulate most Production behavior on the part of leaders, are also situations where the demands for Production are not met by the amount of Production behavior the leader is seen to engage in? In this connection, the possibility should be mentioned again that what is considered *"about right"* may be a shifting value. Perhaps whatever amount of Production behavior is considered "about right" is a larger amount when the situation is such that leaders do engage more frequently in Production behavior. Findings of Likert *et al*, in a study of life insurance companies, tend to confirm this interpretation. Section leaders most concerned with Production and engaged in efforts to increase it, by and large, headed sections whose production achievement was rated lower in comparison with the group norms. Leaders less concerned with production achieved the best ratings.

AGREEMENT AMONG RESPONDENTS DESCRIBING THE SAME LEADER

Variation in reports of observed leader behavior may be assigned to two major sources. First, there is variation due to "real" differences in the "actual" behavior of leaders. Second, there is variation due to differences in the processes of observation and reporting. This second area includes the biases and the limitations of the observation and reporting. One of the goals set in the development of the questionnaire was that of obtaining objective description. By objective description is meant a description that has no variation induced by the second of the two major sources described above. Objective description thus defined, however, is an ideal which can only be approached. At best, we can seek to obtain agreement between all reports of the same behavior. If attention is limited to one method of reporting, such as the use of the LBDQ, the objective of the descriptions can be investigated by determining the agreement between different respondents who describe the same leader's behavior.

Data were gathered by use of the LBDQ concerning the behavior of 6 leaders where each was described by several respondents. Five respondents described the leader of an adult evening school. Five respondents described the one leader of a skilled craft group engaged in the manufacture of prosthetic devices, and 4 respondents described a second leader of a second group within the same manufacturing concern. Six respondents described the leader of an American Legion Post. Five respondents described the leader of a sorority. A group of 14 Ford Motor Company employees described the leader of an administrative office. In every case except one, the leader of the group was also one of the respondents and furnished a description of his own behavior.

There was a highly significant "between leader" variance for Organization and Membership scores. Much less significant agreement between respondent's reports was noted in the case of Domination, Representation, Communication Up, Communication Down, and Recognition. Lack of agreement among respondents, especially in the Domination scores and to some extent in the case of Representation and Recognition, may be due to the restriction of variation in scores, attributable to characteristics of the special sample. However, this explanation would not apply to the Communications dimensions because the variation in these scores was as large for the special sample as for the regular sample.

In general, there seems to be a large component of variation in description which is associated with the specific individual making the observation of a leader's behavior. This would limit the objectivity of the description of a leader's behavior obtained by using the LBDQ.

AN ANALYSIS OF LEADER BEHAVIOR DESCRIPTIONS BY TYPE OF GROUP

To assess the value of a research instrument for the description of leader behavior, it is desirable to know what differences may be expected in its application to different situations. A given research instrument might be very satisfactory for leader behavior description under certain conditions but less satisfactory under others. Some insight into the comparability of descriptions made under different circumstances can be obtained by examining descriptions of leaders from differing "types" of groups. The question "Is there a difference between the way subordinates describe their leaders in 'military' groups as compared with 'educational' groups?" is an example of the problems in this area.

In order to answer some of these questions the descriptions of leader behavior obtained in this study were classified by general types of groups. Four classification categories, which at the common sense level appeared to be fairly obvious, were established as follows:

1. "Education" groups including school administrative staffs, high school and college teacher groups, classes, seminars, and groups of students.
2. "Military" groups including both officer and enlisted men groups.
3. "Occupational" groups including skilled and unskilled worker groups, professional groups, merchandising and clerical groups, government agencies, political groups, social workers, and business groups.
4. "Social" groups including sororities, fraternities, informal social groups, athletic and sports groups, religious groups, political-social groups, Boy and Girl Scouts, summer camps, farming-social, 4-H and FFA, and recreational groups.

It was recognized that in the process of establishing the 4 categories only a minimum of homogeniety within a category and freedom from overlap of categories would be obtained. Both the descriptions made by subordinates and the self-descriptions were classified according to the 4 categories.

The total number of groups in this analysis was fewer than in other analyses. This was due to incomplete information furnished by some respondents, making it impossible to classify some descriptions by type of group.

The analysis of differences in leader behavior, associated with the classification of the groups by type, was carried out in two parts. First, an analysis of the variation of each dimension's scores was made to determine the variance associated with the type of groups, and that associated with differences between leaders of the same type. The second part of the analysis consisted of computing a matrix of the intercorrelations among dimension scores for each type of group. In both analyses, descriptions made by subordinates and by leaders of their own behavior were considered separately.

When subordinates described their leaders, highly significant differences in leader behavior description scores associated with type of group led were found for dimensions Domination, Membership, Representation, Integration, Organization, Communication Down, and Recognition. When leaders described their own behavior, highly significant differences associated with type of group led were found for dimensions Domination, Membership, Representation, and Organization. In the case of both types of description, "occupational" group and "military" group leaders were described as engaging more frequently in Domination behavior than were "social" or "educational" group leaders. Highest mean Membership scores were found for leaders of "social" groups in the case of both types of description. The lowest mean Representation score was found to be associated with leaders of "occupational" groups in the case of both types of description. A low mean Representation score was also earned by leaders of "educational" groups where subordinates were making the description.

Subordinates in "occupational" groups describe their leaders less frequently as engaging in Integration behavior, but subordinates in "social" groups describe their leaders most frequently as engaging in this behavior. Subordinates tended to report leaders of "educational" groups as exhibiting less Organization behavior; however, the leaders themselves reported engaging in Organization behavior more extensively. In both types of description, leaders of "military" groups were observed to engage most frequently in Organization behavior. Subordinates reported Communication Down most frequently in "social" groups and least frequently in "educational" groups. Recognition behavior is least frequently reported by subordinates describing the behavior of leaders of "military" groups.

The findings may be summarized by pointing out some general relations between leader behavior description and type of group led. In "educational" groups, there is reported less Domination, less Representation, less Organization, and less Communication Down than in other groups. In "military" groups, there is found more Domination, more Organization and less Recognition. In "occupational" groups, there is found more Domination, more Membership, more Integration, and more Communication Down than in other groups.

SUMMARY AND DISCUSSION

The preceding sections have presented an analysis of data collected by the administration of the LBDQ to 206 persons who described leaders of groups in which they were members, and to 153 persons who described their own behavior as a leader of a group. This section of the report will attempt to bring together in a general discussion many of the more specific bits of information.

The LBDQ as an instrument for the study of leader behavior has some strong points, but many weaknesses. The strong points include the general ease with which data may be collected by a questionnaire. The advantages of a research instrument which yields data with a minimal investment of time on the part of the research worker and the respondent makes the conduct of larger studies possible. A description of a single leader's behavior might be obtained by use of the questionnaire with an investment of approximately three quarters of an hour's time of a respondent. Other techniques available such as direct observation, interviews, etc., require much more time of either the respondent or trained research personnel.

One rather promising finding with respect to the performance of the LBDQ was the range of responses to most items in the instrument. With the exception of a very few items, respondents did not find any single response to an item to be descriptive of most leaders. It appears that the items in the questionnaire sample areas of behavior where some variation does exist among leaders, or at least in the perceptions respondents have regarding leader behavior.

The weaknesses of the LBDQ become apparent when the dimension classifications for the items of behavior are examined. Not only must the notion that the dimension scores measure unique aspects of leader behavior be rejected, but the probability that all variance in scores is an expression of an evaluation "halo" must be seriously considered. Perhaps the leader's behavior is not being described at all. It may be that all that is obtained from the LBDQ is a relatively expansive over-all evaluation rating stemming from the respondent's judgment of an individual leadership quality. If this be so, it is highly probable that should such an evaluation be desired a much simpler and perhaps more reliable and valid rating form could be constructed.

There is some evidence, however, that such a pessimistic view is not entirely substantiated by the findings. Some of the items have little or no correlation with the over-all evaluation ratings. The dimension total scores do vary in the degree to which they correlate with evaluating ratings. Correlations between dimension total scores and evaluation ratings are not sufficiently high to explain the relatively high reliabilities of the dimension scores. In other words, there is some room for unique variances associated with each dimension. Certain other more specific findings such as the negative correlation between Production total score and Production area evaluation rating suggests some validity of the dimension classifications.

With respect to the problem of evaluation "halo" one must face an almost certainly valid limitation in selecting items to describe leader behavior. Any item which describes any part of the behavior of a leader which is of any consequence in leading a group will necessarily acquire a value component in the perceptions of group members. If this limitation be valid, how can an objective description of leader behavior be obtained by a questionnaire administered to group members? One possible solution lies in the "forced choice" format where items having equal preference value are paired, and where the respondent's task is to choose the one of an equally valued pair as most descriptive of the leader's behavior. The results of the analysis of the data seem to point in the direction of a forced-choice arrangement of items.

A considerable portion of the analysis of data was devoted to a comparison of the questionnaire as an instrument used by a leader for self-description, and as the means for subordinates to describe their leader's behavior.

A number of significant differences was found between the responses to the items when the two types of descriptions were compared. It would appear that a leader's description of his own behavior cannot be considered equivalent to a subordinate's description. Leaders not only tend to avoid making extreme statements about their behavior, especially about less favorable kinds of behavior, but also appear to have different values as to what behavior constitutes "good" leadership.

It is quite evident that there is a large range of individual differences among leaders in how they do their jobs. This is shown by the wide range of responses to practically every item composing the questionnaire. Both subordinates in their descriptions of their leaders, and leaders making descriptions of their own behavior, use frequency levels of "never" through "always" on many items of behavior. A more general answer to the question of "how" leaders do their jobs might be obtained from the interpretation of the factor analysis of the leader behavior dimensions. Here, three major ways of accomplishing the leadership job are found:

1. A leader may stress being a socially acceptable individual in his interactions with other group members.

2. A leader may stress "getting the job done." This would involve emphasis upon group production and concern with problems relative to obtaining the group's objectives.

3. A leader may stress making it possible for members of a group or organization to work together. Emphasis would be on the leader's job as one of a "group catalyst."

These three major "hows" of leader behavior are not mutually exclusive. A given leader may utilize all of them to the same degree or he may use one at the expense of others.

A concluding discussion of this pre-test of the LBDQ would be incomplete without recapitulation of certain limitations inherent in the sampling procedure used. Without doubt, certain types of leadership situations are overemphasized in the sample while other types of situations may be omitted entirely. The problem of what could be considered adequate sampling procedure in attempts to describe leader behavior is difficult to answer. It is probable that leader behavior is substantially related to the type of group in which the leadership occurs as well as to the person engaging in the behavior. Sampling based on securing individuals (1) at random from a defined population, or (2) representatives of a population with respect to known parameters based on individual characteristics would be basically inadequate. Individuals are known to have multiple group membership. A sample based on securing representatives of a population of individuals would not insure that the same sample would be representative of any definite population of groups. Furthermore, it seems that a number of problems lie ahead of a basic problem of sampling in this area. One basic problem is defining a given population of groups. Little is known about the relevant parameters of populations of groups, or even about the descriptive characteristics of an individual group. It seems to the authors that samples of leader behavior which can now be obtained cannot be considered representative of any population. Perhaps in the initial stages of developmental work in these areas we will be forced in sampling to obtain as much variation as possible among the obvious characteristics of the phenomena in which we are interested.

REFERENCES

1. Hemphill, John K. *Situational Factors in Leadership*. Columbus: Ohio State University, Bureau of Educational Research Monograph No. 32, 1949.
2. Stogdill, Ralph M. and Shartle, Carroll L. *Methods in the Study of Administrative Leadership*. Columbus: Ohio State University, Bureau of Business Research Monograph No. 80, 1955.
3. Stogdill, Ralph M., Shartle, Carroll L. and associates. *Patterns of Administrative Performance*. Columbus: Ohio State University, Bureau of Business Research Monograph No. 81, 1956.

III

A FACTORIAL STUDY OF THE LEADER BEHAVIOR DESCRIPTIONS[1]

by

ANDREW W. HALPIN, *University of Chicago*

and

B. JAMES WINER, *Purdue University*

The Leader Behavior Description Questionnaire described in the preceding section was modified for use in the study of Air Force personnel manning bombardment aircraft. The modification consisted of (1) preparing new instructions appropriate to describing the behavior of the aircraft commander, (2) changing the wording of the items, substituting "crew" for "group" and "crew member" for "group member" and (3) reducing the number of dimensions or characteristics to be described.

The number of items in the revised form was reduced from 150 to 130, eliminating 20 items which seemed inappropriate to the air crew situation. Scoring keys were prepared for the following characteristics of leader behavior: Membership (12 items), Communication (22 items), Organization (16 items), Production (12 items), Domination (19 items), Leadership Quality (31 items), Goal Direction (9 items), and Initiative (16 items, some of which were scored on other dimensions). The Leadership Quality dimension was made up of items which, in the previous section, were found to be highly correlated with several different dimensions. Hence, it might be regarded as a good measure of "halo effect" in the description of leadership.

In applying these 8 Keys, 111 of the 130 items were keyed once, 13 appeared in two keys and 6 appeared in none.

The LBDQ was administered to 52 air crews flying B-50 bombers. The leader behavior of the 52 air crew commanders was de-

---

[1] This study was sponsored jointly by the Human Resources Research Laboratories, Department of the Air Force, and The Ohio State University Research Foundation.

scribed by 300 crew members. The 300 descriptions of leader behavior were scored on the 8 keys described above. The intercorrelations among the 8 keys are shown in Table 1. The high intercorrelations among some of the keys indicated that there was considerable overlap between them. A modified Wherry-Doolittle (1) test selection procedure was applied to this rank of intercorrelations and it was found that 5 of the keys would account for almost all the total variance on the 8 keys. The 5 keys (numbers 2, 3, 4, 6 and 8) selected for further analysis and the intercorrelation among them are noted in Table 1. These 5 keys may be regarded as defining 5 factors, but since the keys show intercorrelations significantly greater than zero, they constitute an oblique set of factors.

TABLE 1—Intercorrelations Among Eight Dimension Keys

No.	Dimension (Key)	Dimension (Key)							
		1	2[a]	3[a]	4[a]	5	6[a]	7	8[a]
		r	r	r	r	r	r	r	r
1.	Leadership Quality		.61	.73	.40	.91	.81	.89	.87
2.	Domination[a]	.61		.30	—.18	.57	.61	.44	.49
3.	Organization	.73	.30		.60	.72	.47	.78	.69
4.	Production[a]	.40	—.18	.60		.41	.23	.54	.47
5.	Communication	.91	.57	.72	.41		.79	.84	.80
6.	Membership[a]	.81	.61	.47	.23	.79		.69	.66
7.	Goal Direction	.89	.44	.78	.54	.84	.69		.82
8.	Initiative[a]	.87	.49	.69	.47	.80	.66	.82	
	Mean	88.1	29.1	51.2	28.1	58.3	28.0	25.4	39.6
	Standard Deviation	20.0	9.1	8.3	5.9	11.6	7.8	6.4	8.2

N = 300.
[a] The least highly intercorrelated keys (2, 3, 4, 6 and 8) were selected for use on the factor analysis.

THE FACTOR ANALYSIS

The next step was to compute the correlations between each of the 130 items and each of these five keys. These item-key correlations were used to estimate the factor loadings of the items on each of the keys. These loadings were transformed from a set of oblique to a set of orthogonal reference axes. To accomplish this, a transformation matrix was computed from the matrix of key intercorrelations, and the matrix of oblique factor loadings was multiplied by this transformation matrix to yield the desired matrix of orthogonal factor loadings. The reference axes thus determined were rotated to meaningfulness for the four factors which emerged.

Three additional factors were extracted, but after the completion of rotation, it was found that these three factors accounted for only approximately 6.3 per cent of the variance common to the 7 factors. No meaningful interpretation could be made of the relatively unrepresented factors. Consequently, the additional factors were given no further consideration.

The remaining 4 factors were postulated to account for the intercorrelations. Approximately 32 per cent of the items have one-half or more of their total variance accounted for by the 4 factors. The

TABLE 2—Distribution of Communalities for 130 Items

Communalities	Number of Items	Cumulative Frequency	Cumulative Percentage
80–99	3	3	2.3
60–79	23	26	20.0
40–59	44	70	53.8
20–39	44	114	87.8
0–19	16	130	100.0

TABLE 3—Per Cent of Common Variance Accounted for by Four Factors

Factor Number	Factor Designation	Per Cent of Common Variance
I	Consideration	49.6
II	Initiating Structure	33.6
III	Production Emphasis	9.8
IV	Sensitivity (Social Awareness)	7.0

distribution of communalities is shown in Table 2, where it may be seen that 53.8 per cent of the items have 40 per cent or more of their total variance (communality) accounted for by the 4 factors.

Table 3 shows the per cent of common-factor variance accounted for by the 4 factors. In may be seen that Factors I and II account for 83.2 per cent of the common-factor variance. The factors were identified as Consideration, Initiating Structure, Production Emphasis, and Sensitivity (Social Awareness). Examination of the items with the highest loadings on each factor determined the name assigned to the factor.

Factor I, Consideration, which accounts for 49.6 per cent of the common factor variance is best represented by the items in Table 4.

TABLE 4—Items With High Loadings on Factor I: Consideration

Item	Factor			
	I	II	III	IV[a]
	Factor Loadings			
Does personal favors for crew members	.68	—.05	.06	—.10
Looks out for personal welfare of crew members	.70	.15	.07	—.03
Refuses to explain his actions	—.77	.09	—.04	.14
Treats all crew members as his equal	.81	—.10	—.11	—.12
Is friendly and approachable	.81	.07	.00	.25
Finds time to listen to crew members	.81	.22	.03	—.08

[a] Reflected.

High positive loadings on this factor are associated with behavior indicative of friendship, mutual trust, respect, and warmth in the relationship between the aircraft commander and his crew. High negative loadings appear on items of behavior which indicate that the airplane commander is authoritarian and impersonal in his relations with the members of his crew. Tentatively, this factor has been designated as Consideration. It appears to mean the extent to which the aircraft commander, while carrying out his leadership functions, is considerate of the men on the crew. It does not imply laxity in the performance of his duties.

Factor II, Initiating Structure, is a close second to Factor I in that it accounts for 33.6 per cent of the common-factor variance. This factor is best represented by the items in Table 5.

TABLE 5—Items With High Loadings on Factor II: Initiating Structure

Item	Factor			
	I	II	III	IV[a]
	Factor Loadings			
Asks that crew follow S.O.P.	.03	.60	.15	—.01
Maintains definite standards of performance	.11	.75	.12	.17
Makes sure his part in the crew is understood	.18	.72	.22	.09
Tries out his new ideas on the crew	—.08	.62	.19	.27
Makes his attitude clear to the crew	.15	.63	.14	.22
Assigns crew members to particular tasks	—.07	.57	.20	.16

[a] Reflected.

The behaviors with high positive loadings on this factor are those which indicate that the aircraft commander, to a marked degree, organizes and defines the relationship between himself and the members of his crew. He tends to define the role which he expects each member of the crew to assume, and endeavors to establish well-defined patterns of organization, channels of communication, and ways of getting jobs done. This factor probably represents a basic and unique function of leadership. It is possible that other factors (including Consideration) may represent only facilitating means for accomplishing this end.

Factors I and II, in combination, account for 83.2 per cent of the common-factor variance. Because Factors III and IV account for only 16.8 per cent of this common factor variance, it is not possible at this point to define these factors with the same precision as the first two. This does not imply, however, that Factors III and IV are necessarily any less important than Factors I and II, since the original questionnaire may not have contained adequate samples of behaviors from the areas tapped by Factors III and IV.

Factor III, Production Emphasis, is best represented by the items in Table 6.

TABLE 6—Items With High Loadings on Factor III: Production Emphasis

Item	Factor			
	I	II	III	IV[a]
		Factor Loadings		
Encourages overtime work	—.28	.21	.51	.10
Stresses being ahead of competing crews	.00	.06	.53	.16
Treats crew members like cogs in a machine	—.68	.40	.62	—.03
Schedules the work to be done	.01	.57	.47	—.10
He "needles" crew members for greater effort	—.43	.39	.42	.32

[a] Reflected.

This factor appears to measure a manner of motivating the crew to greater activity by emphasizing the mission or job to be done. Because of the dominance of Factors I and II, there are few "pure" items in this factor.

Factor IV, Sensitivity (Social Awareness), is best represented by the items in Table 7.

Again, as in the case of Factor III, there are relatively few items which have loadings on Factor IV without significant loading on Factors I or II. On the basis of somewhat incomplete data, this factor appears to measure the aircraft commander's sensitivity to and awareness of social interrelationships and pressures existing both

TABLE 7—Items With High Loadings on Factor IV: Sensitivity

Item	Factor			
	I	II	III	IV[a]
	Factor Loadings			
Resists changes in ways of doing things	.28	.25	—.22	**—.49**
Asks for sacrifices for good of entire crew	.16	.27	.02	**.39**
Aware of conflicts when they occur in the crew	.25	.45	—.09	**.65**
"Rides" the crew member who makes a mistake	.14	.32	.46	**—.60**
Waits for the crew to push new ideas	—.07	—.12	.01	**—.32**
Blames the same crew member when anything goes wrong	.17	—.05	.11	**—.53**

[a] Reflected.

inside and outside the crew. It may represent behaviors on the part of the aircraft commander which have often been referred to as "sizing up the situation." This factor does not indicate the extent to which the aircraft commander acts in accordance with these insights, but merely indicates his awareness of social pressures either within the crew or coming from outside the crew. It is important to note that this concept includes also awareness of social pressures which originate outside the crew, and have bearing upon the crew's behavior. There seems, however, to be a distinction between being aware of social pressures and taking appropriate action. Specifically, the aircraft commander's knowledge of the conflicts does not imply that he necessarily takes appropriate action to resolve them.

THE DEVELOPMENT OF SCORING KEYS

The next step was to use the item analysis findings for the construction of new keys. The two major dimensions which had emerged from the factor analysis were Consideration and Initiating Structure. The first objective, therefore, was to develop keys for these two dimensions. Because Factors III and IV contributed little to the common variance and were represented in "pure" form in only relatively few items, no attempt was made at this point to construct keys for these two less clearly delineated dimensions.

Inspection of the correlations of the items with the major dimensions of Consideration and Initiating Structure showed that the degree of association of certain items with one rather than the other of the dimensions was relatively unequivocal, but that in the case of other items, this relationship was not as clear-cut. Consequently, two keys were prepared for each dimension: a "pure" and a "complex." The "pure" key, as the name indicates, is one in which each item has a high correlation with the relevant dimension and a relatively low correlation with the other major dimension. The "complex" key is one in which the items do not possess this same unequivocal relation with the two dimensions, but in which the pattern of factor-loadings for any given item provides a logical basis for assigning the item to a particular dimension key.

Two questions guided the analysis at this point. First, in reviewing the 130 item LBDQ, could the "pure" and "complex" items for the Consideration and Initiating Structure dimensions be amalgamated into a single key for each dimension? Second, with a view to the future objective of constructing a shorter form of the LBDQ, would the choice and number of items in each of the "pure" keys, without the addition of the "complex" items, provide a sufficiently reliable factor key for each of these two dimensions?

Four scoring keys were constructed, consisting of 17 items scored for Consideration "Pure," 11 items scored for Consideration "Complex," 14 items scored for Structure "Pure," and 16 items scored for Structure "Complex." These keys were validated on a new sample of 100 cases, representing members of rather highly selected air crews. The intercorrelations among the 4 new keys are shown in Table 8. The correlation between Consideration "Pure" and Consideration "Complex" is .87, while the correlation between the Structure keys is .72. These correlations are high enough to suggest that the pure and complex keys might be combined if necessary. The correlation of .23 between Consideration "Pure" and Structure "Pure" suggests that these two keys are relatively independent. Lesser independence between these two "Complex" keys is indicated by a correlation of .47 between the two keys. In order to determine the correlation between the combined "pure" and "complex" Consideration keys and the combined "pure" and "complex" Initiating Structure keys, the formula for the correlation of sums was applied to the data in Table 8. This correlation is .42. Thus, the combination of the "complex" items with their respective "pure" items diminishes the independence of the dimension scores (from $r=.23$ to $r=.42$).

The reliability coefficients shown in Table 8 indicate a higher degree of reliability for the "pure" than for the "complex" forms.

TABLE 8—Intercorrelations of "Pure" and "Complex" Keys for Consideration and Initiating Structure: Reliability Coefficients for an Independent Sample of 100 Combat Aircrews

No.	Key	Key			
		1	2	3	4
		r	r	r	r
1.	Consideration "Pure"		.87	.23	.59
2.	Consideration "Complex"	.87		.08	.47
3.	Structure "Pure"	.23	.08		.72
4.	Structure "Complex"	.59	.47	.72	
	Reliability	.95	.89	.83	.79
	Mean	47.1	30.2	43.1	47.3
	Standard Deviation	11.9	7.8	5.5	6.4

The corrected reliability of .95 for Consideration "Pure" and of .83 for Structure "Pure" are high enough to indicate that these keys could be used in short forms of the questionnaires.

Both the intercorrelations among the 4 keys and the data on the reliability of the keys suggest that the "pure" keys alone should be used in constructing new dimension keys.

SHORT FORMS

The next step taken was to construct an 80-item form of the LBDQ. This form consisted of Consideration (15 items), Initiating Structure (15 items), Production Emphasis (25 items), and Social Awareness (25 items). It was hoped, by adding items to the Production Emphasis and Social Awareness Keys, to build up these scales. However, in spite of the attempt to improve them, the Production Emphasis and Social Awareness scales have continued to make only a minor contribution toward measuring the total factor variance. This result may be due in part to the nature of the new items that were added for their measurement in the 80-item form of the questionnaire. Whatever the cause, due to their negligible contribution, they were dropped from further consideration.

The 80-item form of the LBDQ consists, then, of 80 items, only 30 of which are scored. The 15 items scored on the Consideration Key and their factor loadings are shown in Table 9. The 15 items scored on the Initiating Structure Key are shown in Table 10.

It will be noted in Table 9 that the items have high loadings only on Factor I, Consideration. Some of the items have low positive

TABLE 9—Consideration Key: Factor Loadings Derived
From 130-Item Form

Form			Item	Scoring	Factor			
80-Item	130-Item	40-Item			I	II	III	IV
Item Number					Factor Loadings			
1	4	1	He does personal favors for crew members	+	.68	—.05	.06	.10
5	13	3	He does little things to make it pleasant to be a member of the crew	+	.74	—.10	.12	.11
9	18	6	He is easy to understand	+	.69	.12	—.01	.05
13	41	8	He finds time to listen to crew members	+	.81	.22	.03	.08
18	59	12	He keeps to himself	—	—.52	.07	.00	.05
19	74	13	He looks out for the welfare of individual crew members	+	.70	.15	.07	.03
31	87	18	He refuses to explain his actions	—	—.77	.09	—.04	—.14
33	95	20	He acts without consulting the crew	—	—.62	.06	—.02	—.11
34	101	21	He is slow to accept new ideas	—	—.67	—.07	.02	—.13
37	105	23	He treats all crew members as his equals	+	.81	—.10	—.11	.12
37	108	26	He is willing to make changes	+	.74	—.15	.05	.16
45	112	28	He is friendly and approachable	+	.81	.07	.00	.25
51	111	31	He makes crew members feel at ease when talking with him	+	.74	.23	.03	.11
58	114	34	He puts suggestions by the crew into operation	+	.67	.13	.11	—.11
63	124	38	He gets crew approval on important matters before going ahead	+	.63	.02	—.08	.00

loadings on Factors II, III and IV. Other items have negative loadings on Factors II, III or IV. Items with both positive and negative loadings on Factors II, III and IV were included with the aim of suppressing or cancelling out the effect of these three factors. It may be seen in Table 10 that the same principle was followed less successfully in selecting items for measuring Structure.

In the final form of the LBDQ, constructed recently, the number of items was reduced to 40, with 15 items for measuring Consideration, 15 items for measuring Structure, and 10 buffer items to maintain the "tone" of the questionnaire provided by the items intended to measure Factors III and IV. The item numbers of the items in the 40-item form are shown in Tables 9 and 10.

For a sample of 100 of the 80-item questionnaires, the odd-even estimates of reliability are .87 for Consideration and .75 for Initiating Structure. When the Spearman-Brown formula is applied to correct

TABLE 10—Initiating Structure Key: Factor Loadings Derived From 130-Item Form

Form			Item	Scoring	Factor			
80—Item	130—Item	40—Item			I	II	III	IV
Item Number					Factor Loadings			
2	3	2	He makes his attitude clear to the crew	+	.15	.63	.14	—.22
6	9	4	He tries out his new ideas in the crew	+	—.08	.62	.19	—.27
10	11	7	He rules with an iron hand	+	—.66	.61	.27	—.22
14	14	9	He criticizes poor work	+	—.20	.55	.17	—.31
17	17	11	He speaks in a manner not to be questioned	+	—.05	.47	.14	—.10
21	31	14	He assigns crew members to particular tasks	+	—.07	.57	.20	—.16
25	24	16	He works without a plan	—	—.32	—.58	—.04	—.06
26	56	17	He maintains definite standards of performance	+	.11	.75	.12	.17
35	117	22	He emphasizes meeting deadlines	+	.18	.48	.05	—.25
38	121	24	He encourages the use of uniform procedures	+	.19	.66	.26	—.13
42	128	27	He makes sure his part in the crew is understood by members	+	.17	.72	.22	—.09
46	39	29	He asks that crew members follow standard operating procedures	+	.03	.60	.15	.01
52	129	32	He lets crew members know what is expected of them	+	.29	.58	.11	—.18
59	46	35	He sees to it that crew members are working up to capacity	+	—.12	.71	.34	—.12
64	102	39	He sees to it that the work of crew members is coordinated	+	.44	.60	.18	—.05

for attenuation, the reliabilities for these keys become .93 and .86, respectively. The 15-item keys are thus shown to exhibit usefully high reliabilities.

There remains the question as to whether or not complete independence was achieved between the Consideration and Structure scales. In one sample of 29 air crew commanders described by 201 crew members a correlation of .52 was found between the Consideration and Initiating Structure scores. When the same air crew commanders were later described on a different air base the correlation between the two scales was .45. For another sample of 249 aircraft commanders a correlation of .38 was found between the two scales. Although the factor analysis showed Consideration and Structure to be orthogonal factors, uncorrelated factor scores could not be obtained since few items were factorially pure. Some indi-

TABLE 11—Analysis of Variance of Consideration Scores of 29 Air Crew Commanders Described by 201 Crew Members

Source of Variation	Sum of Squares	Degrees of Freedom	Estimate of Variance	F Ratio
Between Crews	11,409.27	28	407.47	4.07[a]
Within Crews	17,225.70	172	100.15	
Total	28,634.97	200		

[a] Significant at the .01 level.

viduals exhibit both forms of behavior. Reference to Table 10 shows that the items for the measurement of Initiating Structure show moderately high loadings on Factors I, III and IV. Initiating Structure appears to represent a complex form of behavior, difficult to measure independently of other behavioral dimensions. In addition, the great variety of demands imposed by military life and operating conditions would appear to preclude the absolute separation of Consideration and Initiating Structure.

A further question remains relative to the extent to which several persons describing the same leader, tend to describe him in the same terms. In the samples under discussion, each air crew commander was described by four or more crew members. It has been found in several samples of subjects that different subordinates describing the same leader tend to describe him in similar terms. However, different leaders are not described as similar. Results of the analysis of variance among the description scores of 29 air crew commanders described by 201 crew members are shown in Tables 11 and 12. The variance in the descriptions of different leaders is found to be significantly greater than the variance in description of the same leader.

Comparison of Tables 11 and 12 reveals a tendency toward greater agreement in describing the air crew commander's behavior with respect to Consideration than in describing his behavior with regard to Initiating Structure. In view of the significant F ratios

TABLE 12—Analysis of Variance of Initiating Structure Scores of 29 Air Crew Commanders Described by 201 Crew Members

Source of Variation	Sum of Squares	Degrees of Freedom	Estimate of Variance	F Ratio
Between Crews	4,591.77	28	163.99	2.00[a]
Within Crews	14,118.60	172	82.09	
Total	18,710.37	200		

[a] Significant at the .01 level.

for both dimensions, it was concluded that the crew mean Consideration and crew mean Initiating Structure scores could be used as indices for describing the leader behavior of the air crew commander as perceived by his crew.

THE RELATION OF LEADER BEHAVIOR DESCRIPTION SCORES TO OTHER MEASURES

Ratings of leadership effectiveness were available for the sample of 29 air crew commanders. These ratings were made by the administrative superiors of the commanders. Ratings were made on technical competence, effectiveness in working with other crew members, performance under stress, and the like. The correlations between these effectiveness ratings by superiors and the leader behavior of the air crew commanders as described by their subordinates are shown in Table 13. The last item in this table is a crew satisfaction index. This is on evaluation by the crew members of their satisfaction with the leadership of the air crew commander.

It will be seen in Table 13 that Consideration is correlated negatively with all the effectiveness ratings by superiors. This negative relationship is enhanced when Initiating Structure is partialled out. It is apparent that Consideration is not perceived as a form of beha-

TABLE 13—Correlations and Partial Correlations Between Effectiveness Ratings by Superiors and Leader Behavior Descriptions by Subordinates for 29 Air Crew Commanders

Effectiveness Rating	Consideration Score	Structure Score	Consideration with Structure Partialled out	Structure with Consideration Partialled out
	r	r	r	r
Technical Competence	—.22	.19	—.38[a]	.36[a]
Effectiveness of Working with Other Crew Members	—.13	.27	—.33	.40[a]
Conformity to Standard Operating Procedures	—.25	.32	—.52[b]	.54[b]
Performance Under Stress	—.12	.16	—.24	.26
Attitude and Motivation to be Effective	—.34	.16	—.50[b]	.42[a]
Over-all Effectiveness as a Combat Crew Member	—.23	.28	—.46[a]	.48[b]
Crew's Satisfaction Index	.64[b]	.35	.57[b]	—.03

[a] Significant at the .05 level.
[b] Significant at the .01 level.

vior which contributes directly toward leadership effectiveness. Initiating Structure is correlated positively with all the effectiveness ratings, significantly so for 4 items when Consideration is partialled out. Initiating Structure as described by subordinates is associated with leadership effectiveness as rated by superiors. Crew satisfaction, however, is more highly related to Consideration than to Initiating Structure. Consideration would, thus, appear to be a form of behavior which contributes toward crew morale rather than making a direct contribution to effectiveness.

SUMMARY

A Leader Behavior Description Questionnaire consisting of 130 items was administered to crew members who described air crew commanders. A factor analysis of the intercorrelations among 8 hypothesized dimensions of leader behavior resulted in the emergence of 4 factors. These factors were identified as Consideration, Initiating Structure, Production Emphasis, and Social Awareness.

Two factors, Consideration and Initiating Structure, accounted for 83 per cent of the total factor variance. Attempts to improve the contribution of the two remaining factors by increasing the number of items for their measurement proved unsuccessful. Efforts were therefore concentrated upon the task of developing the best possible short scales for describing Consideration and Initiating Structure.

In an 80-item form of the questionnaire, only the 15 items for measuring consideration and the 15 items for measuring Structure were keyed and scored. The reliabilities of these short keys were found to be satisfactorily high for practical use. The two scales are correlated to a moderate degree, but are sufficiently independent to permit the use of the Consideration and Initiating Structure scales as measures of different kinds of behavior. Different persons describing the same leader show significant similarity in their descriptions.

Consideration tends to be correlated negatively with leadership effectiveness ratings by superiors, while Initiating Structure is positively related to effectiveness ratings. Consideration is more highly related than Initiating Structure to an index of crew satisfaction.

REFERENCES
1. Wherry, R. J. and Winer, B. J. A Method for Factoring Large Numbers of Items. Psychometrica, 1953, *18*, 161–179.

IV

THE LEADER BEHAVIOR AND EFFECTIVENESS OF AIRCRAFT COMMANDERS[1]

Andrew W. Halpin
University of Chicago

What aspects of leader behavior are most important for the effective combat performance of aircraft commanders? That the commanders of medium bombardment aircraft vary in their leadership style is evident from even casual observation. But to note differences in leadership style is of doubtful practical value unless we can identify meaningful dimensions by which such differences may be reliably described. Furthermore, it behooves us to demonstrate that such differences have a bearing upon the commander's combat performance. In other words, we should seek to discover the relationship between *descriptions* of what the leader does and independent *evaluations* of the effectiveness of his leadership.

The source of such evaluations is determined by the aircraft commander's position within a larger organizational structure. He is the leader of a primary, face-to-face group—the crew, but is at the same time responsible to squadron and wing superiors. His position, therefore, confronts him with two sets of obligations: responsibility to his administrative superiors for the accomplishment of the crew's mission, and responsiveness to the crew in respect to the means by which this end is achieved. As the leader of a primary group imbedded within a larger hierarchical organization, the aircraft commander's performance is thus under double scrutiny—by his superiors, and by his crew. The expectations imposed upon him from these two sources are not necessarily the same. Accordingly, in examining the pertinence of differences in leadership style, we must be careful to take into account evaluations of the commander's performance derived from both these sources.

[1] This study was sponsored jointly by the Human Resources Research Laboratories, Department of the Air Force, and The Ohio State University Research Foundation.

The design is straightforward, and involves three kinds of variables: (1) descriptions of the aircraft commander's behavior by the members of his crew, (2) evaluations of his performance by his administrative superiors, and (3) evaluations of the commander in terms of sociometric ratings secured from his crew. The procedure is to determine the relationship between the descriptions (1) and the two sets of evaluations (2 and 3).

Hypotheses

In order to facilitate and insure the fulfillment of role requirements, there is developed within every formal and hierarchical organization, some system of rewards and punishments. The larger the organization, and the greater the demand for the interchangeability of the incumbents of any given position, the less can the institution tolerate deviations from specified role requirements. If Initiating Structure behavior be viewed as an index of the degree to which any given commander is successful in fulfilling the institutionally established requirements of his role, then one might expect that this behavior would be rewarded. *Specifically, we would expect squadron and wing superiors to rate favorably the performance of those commanders who show high Initiating Structure behavior. This is the first hypothesis to be tested in the present investigation.*

But we have noted at the outset that the leader of any primary group imbedded within a larger organizational structure, is confronted by two sets of obligations: to his superiors, and to his crew. Responsiveness to the crew refers to responsiveness in terms of interpersonal relations. The dimension of Consideration would appear to be an index of the degree to which the commander is responsive to his crew, in terms not of institutional roles or goals, but rather in regard to interpersonal needs. *This leads to the second hypothesis to be tested: that crews will prefer as aircraft commanders those leaders who are high in Consideration behavior.* The two dimensions may be viewed as contributing primarily to two different kinds of group objectives. Initiating Structure is directed principally at the achievement of the formal goals of the group, i.e., success on missions, whereas Consideration behavior is related essentially to the maintenance or strengthening of the group itself.

Inasmuch as *both* group achievement and group maintenance

are important, it is not sufficient for us to examine singly the relationship of each of the two leader behavior dimensions to performance criteria. We may assume that the more effective leader is the commander who simultaneously can contribute to both group objectives. *From this we posit our third hypothesis—that commanders who are rated highest by their superiors on "Overall Effectiveness in Combat" are those who score above the mean on both leader behavior dimensions, and that the commanders who are rated lowest by their superiors on this same criterion are those who score below the mean on both dimensions.*

If these hypotheses are supported by the data, we shall be provided with a firmer basis upon which to build our leader selection and training programs.

The Sample and Primary Data

The sample is comprised of 89 commanders of B-29 aircraft assigned to the Far East Air Force and engaged in flying combat missions over Korea. Data were gathered on these commanders in Japan during the summer of 1951. There are three sets of data pertinent to the present study: (1) scores on the Air Force adaptation of the Leader Behavior Description Questionnaire on which the crew members described the behavior of their respective commanders, (2) ratings of the commander's performance secured from his squadron and wing administrative superiors, and (3) sociometric ratings of the commanders by their respective crews. Hemphill and Sechrest (4) have described the collection of the data and the analysis of the criterion data. The data for the present study are described in greater detail by Halpin (2, 3).

The Leader Behavior Description Questionnaire

The Leader Behavior Description Questionnaire (LBDQ) as adapted for the Air Force investigation is an 80-item questionnaire in multiple choice format. Only 30 of the items are scored. The Consideration and the Initiating Structure keys are each comprised of 15 items.

For a sample of 670 crew members describing their 93 respective aircraft commanders, odd-even estimates of the reliability of the keys were made. For the Consideration key, the estimate of reliability is .85, which when corrected by the Spearman-Brown formula is raised to .92. Correspondingly, the estimated reliability of the Initiating Structure key is .71, which is raised to .83 by the Spearman-Brown correction.

For the study proper, data were used for only 89 of the 93 commanders. The other 4 cases were eliminated because in each instance Leader Behavior Descriptions were obtained from less than four members of the crew. Hence, the Leader Behavior Description data are based upon the responses of 662 crew members describing their 89 respective aircraft commanders. The number of descriptions per commander ranged from 4 to 10, with a mean of 7.4 and standard deviation of 2.1. That the crew members tend to agree in the description of their respective commanders is shown by "between vs. within crew" F ratios significant at the .01 level in the case of each of the two dimensions. Epsilon, the unbiased correlation ratio, provides an index to the degree of this agreement. For the Consideration dimension, epsilon is .54; for the Initiating Structure dimension, it is .41.

For each of the 89 crews, the scores by which the crew members described their aircraft commander's leadership behavior were averaged separately for each of the two dimensions. These crew mean scores will be treated as the Consideration and the Initiating Structure scores ascribed to the 89 commanders by their respective crews. The mean Consideration score is 40.3 with a standard deviation of 8.3; the mean Initiating Structure, 40.0 with a standard deviation of 5.1. The correlation between these two sets of ascribed scores is .51.

Ratings by Administrative Superiors

An Individual Criterion Rating Form was developed for the evaluation of individual crew members including commanders. To obtain these ratings, staff officers at the squadron and wing level were interviewed individually. Each rater was asked to select from a roster those persons with whom he was sufficiently well acquainted to make an equitable rating. The interviewer then asked the rater to evaluate each man on a nine-point scale in respect to seven different characteristics. The ratings were recorded along with a verbatim record of comments made by the rater about the performance of the ratee. No rater was requested to evaluate any men with whose performance he was only vaguely familiar.

Ratings were obtained on 87 of the 89 aircraft commanders in the sample. Fourteen of these 87 were evaluated by one superior, 48 by two, and 25 by three. Each commander was evaluated in respect to the following characteristics:

1. *Technical competence:* The degree of competence in performing his crew duties.
2. *Effectiveness in working with other crew members:* The degree to which the individual is effective in coordinating his work with other crew members, or the degree to which he works as an effective team member.
3. *Conformity to Standard Operating Procedure (SOP):* The degree to which he performs his duties in the prescribed manner.
4. *Performance under stress:* The degree to which he is able to maintain a high level of performance under high stress conditions, i.e., in the face of enemy opposition, or when called upon for long hours of duty.
5. *Attitude and motivation:* The degree to which the crew as a unit displays enthusiasm or eagerness for effective combat performance.
6. *Overall effectiveness:* The degree to which the individual displays an overall effectiveness as a member of a combat crew.

A 9-point scale was used by the raters in evaluating commanders on each of the 6 performance characteristics. The ratings on each characteristic which the commander received from different superiors were averaged, and these averages were used as the commanders' "scores" on the Individual Criterion Rating Form. One would expect these ratings to be intercorrelated. A factor analysis of these ratings for the aircraft commander position identified three factors: Overall Effectiveness, Technical Competence—but without correspondingly high "overall effectiveness," and Conformity to Administrative Requirements.

Sociometric Ratings by the Crew

In order to obtain an evaluation of the aircraft commander as perceived by the members of his crew, two kinds of measures have been used: three scores derived from a set of five sociometric rating scales; and a Satisfaction Index indicating the crew's satisfaction with the incumbent aircraft commander. These measures will be discussed in turn.

The five sociometric rating questions were incorporated within a larger Crew Rating Form administered to all crew members including the commander. For each question, a 9-point scale was used, with 5 of the points anchored by brief verbal descriptions. These sociometric questions are listed below:

1. How much confidence do you have in each member of your crew?

1	2	3	4	5	6	7	8	9
None		Little		Average		Great Deal		Highest

2. How would you rate each crew member as your friend or possible friend?

1	2	3	4	5	6	7	8	9
I can't stand to be around him		I would rather not associate		At present he is just another guy		I enjoy being with him		I try to be with him more often

3. How proficient do you think each member of your crew is?

1	2	3	4	5	6	7	8	9
Very poor		Poor		Fair		Good		Very Good

4. Rate the morale of each man in this crew.

1	2	3	4	5	6	7	8	9
Very poor		Poor		Average		Good		Excellent

5. To what extent will each crew member go out of his way to help another crew member in performing his duties?

1	2	3	4	5	6	7	8	9
Never goes out of his way		Seldom goes out of his way to help another		Sometimes will go out of his way and sometimes won't		Will generally go out of his way to help another		Always goes out of his way

These five scales will be referred to as ratings of: (1) Confidence, (2) Friendship, (3) Proficiency, (4) Morale, and (5) Cooperation.

Each crew member rated each other member of the crew except himself. For any given man, the rating assigned to him is the average of the ratings he received from his fellow crew members. For the purpose of the present study, we shall be concerned only with the mean ratings received by the aircraft commanders.

As might have been expected, these ratings were highly intercorrelated. Upon factor analysis of the matrix, two factors were identified as sufficiently independent to permit a meaningful interpretation. In this solution, only 16 per cent communality was obtained for the ratings on morale. Consequently the morale ratings are treated separately. The interrelationships among the other four ratings were such as to suggest the advisability of a straightforward combining of the scores into two groups. Accordingly, we have computed mean scores for each of the five ratings and have then reduced the five scores to the folowing three:

Score I—Confidence and Proficiency
Score II—Friendship and Cooperation
Score III—Morale

Each of these represents the crew's pooled evaluation of the aircraft commander in respect to these particular characteristics.

Satisfaction Index

The second kind of sociometric rating of the commander secured from the crew was the Satisfaction Index. On one of the questions of the Crew Rating Form, the respondents were asked: "If you could make up a crew from among the crew members in your squadron, whom would you choose for each crew position?" The ratio between the number of choices the incumbent commander received and the number of choices possible was used as an index of the crew's satisfaction with his leadership.

An index of 100 means that in response to this question, all the crew members chose their present aircraft commander. Conversely, an index of 0 means that none of the members chose the incumbent commander. For 88 commanders, the scores on this crew Satisfaction Index ranged from 0 to 100, with a mean of 75 and a standard deviation of 29.

Initiating Structure Scores and Superiors' Ratings

The correlations between the Consideration and the Initiating Structure scores ascribed to the aircraft commanders and their ratings on the other variables are presented in Table 1. One notes, in general, that none of the ratings by superiors, whether in the form of individual ratings or of factor scores correlates significantly with

TABLE 1—Correlations Between Ascribed Consideration and Initiating Structure Scores and Ratings of Commanders by Superiors, and by Crew Members With Means and Standard Deviations for the Respective Variables

Ratings by Superiors and Crew Members	N	Dimension		Mean	SD
		Consideration	Initiating Structure		
Ratings by Superiors		r	r		
Technical Competence	87	.09	.30	5.5	2.5
Effectiveness in Working with Others	87	.18	.28	5.2	2.3
Conformity to Standard Procedures	87	—.03	.32	4.7	2.3
Performance Under Stress	87	.18	.32	6.3	1.9
Attitude and Motivation	87	.03	.29	5.1	2.1
Over-all Effectiveness	87	.17	.30	5.3	2.4
Factor I. Over-all Effectiveness	86	.17	.25	5.5	2.3
Factor II: Lack of Motivation	86	.14	.14	5.1	2.2
Factor III: Conformity to Administrative Requirements	86	—.18	.10	3.6	1.5
Ratings by Crew					
Score I: Confidence and Proficiency	84	.69	.68	7.7	1.5
Score II: Friendship and Cooperation	84	.84	.51	5.7	1.9
Score III: Morale	84	.27	.28	5.2	1.9
Satisfaction Index	88	.75	.47	75.0	28.7

r = .21 is significant at the .05 level.
r = .27 is significant at the .01 level.

the Consideration scores, but that conversely all the ratings on individual criteria by superiors yield correlations significant at the .01 level with the Initiating Structure scores. The consistency in the magnitude of these correlations is probably a function of a general rater halo, for the only one of the three factor scores derived from these ratings by superiors which correlates significantly with the Initiating Structure scores is Factor I—Overall Effectiveness. This correlation of .25 is significant at the .05 level. On the whole, therefore, the superiors rate favorably those aircraft commanders who are perceived by their crews as high in Initiating Structure. This supports the first of the two hypotheses which provided the impetus for the present study.

Consideration Scores and Ratings by Crew Members

The second hypothesis, that the Consideration scores would be correlated with favorable ratings of the commander by the members of his own crew, is also supported. This is especially the case in two instances: The correlation of .75 with the Satisfaction index, and the correlation of .84 with Score II derived from the sociometric ratings on "Friendship and Cooperation." One observes, however, that correlations significant at the .01 level are also obtained with the Initiating Structure scores. In the case of Scores I and III, for example, the correlations are of the same magnitude for each of the leader behavior dimensions. But with the other two variables, the Satisfaction Index and Score II, the difference between the Consideration correlation and the correlation with the Initiating Structure scores is statistically significant. The magnitude of these two correlations and the size of the difference between each of these and the corresponding Initiating Structure correlations is sufficient, however, to support the hypotheses of a high positive relationship between the Consideration scores and the ratings by the crew.

"Half-Crew" vs. "Total Crew" Scores

Regarding the correlations between the Leader Behavior Description Questionnaire scores and the evaluations of the leader by his own crew members, the question may be raised as to the extent to which these correlations are contaminated by the fact that both measures were obtained from the same respondents. This question was investigated in the case of the Satisfaction Index. As previously noted, the correlations given in Table 1 between this Index and the Leader Behavior Description scores were computed with data obtained from the same crew members. Specifically, the Index was the ratio of (a) the number of choices which the commander did receive from all the members of his crew, to (b) the number of choices which he maximally could have obtained from the same members. From the same respondents, the ascribed Consideration and Initiating Structure scores of each commander were computed by averaging, for each dimension, the scores by which all the members of his crew described him. In order to investigate possible contamination due to the fact that both sets of scores had been obtained from the same respondents, the Satisfaction Index and the Leader Behavior Description scores were each computed from a different half of the crew. For example, in one crew the Satisfaction Index was computed on the basis of the responses of the "odd" members of the crew; with the Consideration and the Initiating Structure scores computed solely from the responses of the "even" members of the crew. In the next crew, the Satisfaction Index was computed from the responses of the "even" members, and the Leader Behavior Description scores from the responses of the "odd" members. In alternating this combination as we went through the list of crews, care was taken to balance, in respect to officer vs. airmen personnel, the number of responses upon which the score for each variable was computed. These sets of "half-crew" scores were then correlated. For 87 crews, the correlation between the Satisfaction Index and the Consideration scores is .51 (significant at the .01 level), and between this index and the Initiating Structure scores, .22 (significant at the .05 level). The corresponding correlations computed from the full-crew scores are .75 and .47, respectively. Thus a parallel relationship obtains between the Leader Behavior Description scores and the Satisfaction Index whether the scores be based upon the half or the whole crew data. The difference between the respective half and whole crew correlations indicates the extent to which the common source of repondents may be viewed as a contaminating factor. In respect to the issue of the present inquiry, however, the important point to be noted is that even with these half-crew scores a correlation as high as .51 is obtained between the Consideration scores and the Satisfaction Index.

"Crew Acceptance" Cluster

The two highest correlations in Table 1 are those of the Consideration scores with the "Friendship and Cooperation" scores (.84), and with the Satisfaction Index (.75). The correlation between the Satisfaction Index and the "Friendship and Cooperation" scores is, in turn, .81. Here, then, is a consistent cluster of relationships. *The aircraft commanders whom the men perceive as most considerate are those whom they rate highest on "Friendship and Cooperation," and whom they clearly prefer as their aircraft commanders.* In general, the three variables in this cluster appear to measure the crew's acceptance of the aircraft commander as a person. It therefore is of some interest to examine the relationships between the variables in this cluster and the three factor scores derived from the ratings of the commander by his superiors. These correlations are presented in Table 2.

Only one of these correlations is significant, that between the

TABLE 2—Correlations of Variables in Crew Acceptance Cluster With Factor Scores Derived From Superiors' Ratings of Aircraft Commanders

Variables in Crew Acceptance Cluster	N	Superior's Ratings		
		I Over-all Effectiveness	II Lack of Motivation	III Conformity to Administrative Requirements
		r	r	r
Consideration	86	.17	.14	—.18
Satisfaction Index	85	.23	.17	—.13
Friendship and Cooperation	89	.14	.16	.10

$r = .21$ is significant at the .05 level.

superiors' ratings of the commanders' over-all effectiveness and the index we have used to express the crew's satisfaction with its commander. Apart from this single correlation indicating only approximately 5 per cent of variance common to the two variables, there are only chance relationships between the measures of the commander's acceptance by his crew and the ratings he receives from his superiors.

Up to this point of our analysis, we have examined the relationship between the criteria and each leader behavior dimension taken separately. In general, we found that high Initiating Structure behavior is associated with favorable ratings by administrative superiors, and that high Consideration is associated with acceptance by the crew members. These findings support the first two hypotheses which we have set out to test.

High vs. Low Scores on Both Dimensions

The third hypothesis proposed was that the aircraft commanders rated highest by their superiors on "Overall Effectiveness in Combat" would be those scoring above the mean on both leader behavior dimensions, and that the commanders rated lowest by their superiors on this same criterion would be those scoring below the mean on both dimensions. To test this hypothesis, we first determined appropriate cutting points in the distribution of the ratings the aircraft commanders received from their superiors on "Overall Effectiveness in Combat." It was decided that the upper and lower 15 per cent of the distribution clearly identified two groups of commanders: those rated high on Overall Effectiveness ($N = 13$) and those rated low

($N = 12$). For each of these groups taken separately, the Consideration and the Initiating Structure scores were plotted into the four quadrants defined by coordinates corresponding to the means of the two leader behavior dimensions. These scatterplots for the high and low groups on Overall Effectiveness are presented in Table. 3.

TABLE 3—Relation Between Consideration and Iniating Structure Scores of Aircraft Commanders Rated High or Low in Effectiveness by Superiors

Initiating Structure	Consideration			
	Below Mean	N	Above Mean	N
Above Mean	Effectiveness High	4	Effectiveness High	8
	Low	2	Low	2
Below Mean	Effectiveness High	1	Effectiveness High	0
	Low	6	Low	2

The cell entries in the upper left hand quadrant of the table do not differ significantly from each other. Nor do the entries in the two respective lower right hand quadrants. On the other hand, when we compare the two groups of commanders with respect to those high on *both* leader behavior dimensions and those low on *both* dimensions, we obtain the relationship summarized in Table 4.

TABLE 4—Number of Aircraft Commanders Scoring High or Low in Effectiveness and Scoring Above the Mean or Below the Mean in Both Leader Behavior Dimensions

Effectiveness Rating	Number Below Mean on Both Consideration and Structure	Number Above Mean on Both Consideration and Structure
Upper 15 per cent	1	8
Lower 15 per cent	6	2

Fisher's (1) method for the exact treatment of 2×2 tables was applied to the data in Table 4. The probability of occurrence of frequencies as deviant or more deviant from the null hypothesis than those obtained is less that .03. This indicates that aircraft commanders who are rated high by their superiors on Overall Effectiveness tend to score above the mean on both leader behavior dimensions, whereas the commanders rated low by their superiors tend to score below the mean on *both* dimensions. Here then, is support for the third hypothesis. The evidence thus indicates that the effective aircraft commander is not the one who engages in one form of leader behavior at the expense of the other, but rather is the leader whose behavior is above average in respect to both the Consideration and the Initiating Structure dimensions.

Discussion

Two dimensions of the leader behavior of aircraft commanders have been studied. For the sample of 89 aircraft commanders studied, the correlation between these two dimensions is .51. Recognizing that the crux of leadership behavior lies in how it is evaluated by the men with whom the leader must deal, we have determined the relationship between the commanders' behavior in respect to these two dimensions and the evaluation of his combat performance by his superiors and his crew members. In general, we find that the ratings of the commander by his superiors are correlated significantly with the Initiating Structure scores, and that his ratings by his crew members are correlated highest with the Consideration scores.

Both dimensions are integral components of a leader's behavior. But in evaluating the aircraft commander's performance, his superiors and his crew each selectively perceives one dimension as more important than the other. Yet in neither case is the second of the dimensions viewed adversely. For the crew, if the commander is Considerate, then a moderately high degree of Initiating Structure behavior is acceptable. For the superiors, although the prime requirement is that the aircraft commander be strong in Initiating Structure, a moderately high degree of Consideration behavior is acceptable. *In short, our findings suggest that to select a leader who is likely to satisfy both his crew and his superiors, we do best by choosing an aircraft commander who is above average on both leader behavior dimensions.*

V

THE OBSERVED LEADER BEHAVIOR AND IDEAL LEADER BEHAVIOR OF AIRCRAFT COMMANDERS AND SCHOOL SUPERINTENDENTS[1]

ANDREW W. HALPIN
University of Chicago

The purpose of this study is to determine the relation between a leader's ideal (how he thinks he should behave as a leader) and his actual leadership behavior as observed by his subordinates. The sample consists of two groups of subjects, 64 educational administrators and 132 aircraft commanders.

The sample of 64 administrators was drawn from two sources: superintendents studied in a survey of Ohio public schools (3), and 13 superintendents and principals who participated in a graduate seminar on "Leadership for Educational Administrators."

The 132 aircraft commanders were in charge of B-50 and B-29 crews. The composition and structure of the crews on the two types of aircraft are essentially similar. The commanders of the two types of crews do not differ significantly in leader behavior or leadership ideology, and hence were combined into a single sample.

The 64 administrators described their own ideal behavior on the Leader Behavior Dimension Questionnaire—"Ideal." They were also described by 428 members of their staffs. An average of 6.7 descriptions was obtained for each administrator. The 132 commanders answered the LBDQ—"Ideal," and were described on the LBDQ "Real" by 1,099 crew members. An average of 8.3 descriptions was obtained for the commanders.

Both the "Real" and "Ideal" forms of the Leader Behavior Description Questionnaire (LBDQ) were scored on each of two dimensions: Consideration and Initiating Structure. The leader's own scores on the "Ideal" form provided a measure of his ideology in

[1] Reprinted in part from the *Harvard Educational Review*, 1955, 25, 18–32.

respect to the two dimensions. Descriptions by subordinates on the LBDQ—"Real" served as an index of his real behavior as perceived by members of his group.

An analysis of variance design was used to determine whether members tend to agree in describing the same leader. For both dimensions and for both groups, F ratios significant at the .01 level were obtained, indicating that subordinates differ more in describing different leaders than in describing the same leader. An unbiased correlation ratio (epsilon) was also computed to show to what extent group members agreed in describing the same leader. These ratios for Consideration are .49 for administrators and .61 for commanders. The ratios for Initiating Structure are .49 for administrators and .44 for commanders.

Leaders in these military and educational organizations differ in their behavior as described by their subordinates (Table 1). They

TABLE 1—Means, Standard Deviations, and t Ratios of Mean Differences in Leader Behavior of 64 Administrators and 132 Commanders

Leader Behavior	Commanders		Administrators		
	M	SD	M	SD	t[a]
Consideration					
Real	39.7	8.0	44.7	6.0	—4.38
Ideal	48.7	5.3	52.4	3.9	—4.93
t Ratio	11.7		9.0		
Structure					
Real	40.9	4.9	37.9	4.4	4.11
Ideal	51.0	4.6	43.8	6.4	8.97
t Ratio	18.5		7.3		

[a] All reported t's are significant at the .001 level of confidence.

also differ in their leadership ideology. Aircraft commanders exhibit more Initiating Structure and less Consideration than educational administrators. The differences are significant at the .001 level of confidence for both "real" and "ideal" behavior.

Both groups of leaders indicate that they should show more Consideration and Initiating Structure than their followers describe them as doing. These differences are all significant at the .001 level of confidence.

As indicated in Table 2, the "real" behavior of the subjects does not conform to their "ideal" behavior. The highest correlation (.34) is that between the "real" and the "ideal" structuring behavior of educational administrators.

TABLE 2—Correlations Among Descriptions of "Real" and "Ideal" Leader Behavior for 64 Administrators and 132 Commanders

Variables Correlated	Commanders	Administrators
	r	r
Consideration "Real" vs. Consideration "Ideal"	.17a	.09
Structure "Real" vs. Structure "Ideal"	.14	.34b
Structure "Real" vs. Consideration "Real"	.45b	.13
Structure "Ideal" vs. Consideration "Ideal"	.29b	.22

a Significant at the .05 level.
b Significant at the .01 level.

It may also be observed in Table 2 that there is very little relationship ($r = .13$) between the Consideration and Initiating Structure descriptions of educational administrators. Aircraft commanders who are described as high in Consideration tend to be described as high in Initiating Structure. The correlation is .45. The "ideal" Consideration and Initiating Structure scores are also somewhat more highly correlated for commanders than for administrators.

SUMMARY

The Leader Behavior Description Questionnaire was administered to 64 educational administrators and 132 aircraft commanders. The subjects described their own "ideal" behavior as leaders. The "real" behavior of each subject was also described by several subordinates on a separate form of the questionnaire. Scores were obtained for each subject, representing his Consideration behavior, "real" and "ideal," as well as his Initiating Structure behavior, "real" and "ideal."

It was found that the mean scores of administrators exceed the mean score of commanders for Consideration, but that the reverse is true for Initiating Structure. These differences are all significant at the .001 level for both "real" and "ideal" scores.

The Consideration behavior of educational administrators is described as relatively independent of their Initiating Structure behavior. There is a greater tendency among aircraft commanders for those who exhibit Consideration also to exhibit Structuring behavior.

Only a low relationship was found between the "real" scores and the "ideal." The highest correlation was that between the "real" and "ideal" Structuring behavior of educational administrators. *It may be said, in general, that a leader's beliefs about how he should behave as a leader are not highly associated with his behavior as described by his followers.* On the basis of these findings, personnel workers engaged in leadership training programs should be especially wary about accepting trainees' statements of how they should behave as evidence of parallel changes in their actual behavior.

REFERENCES

1. Halpin, A. W. The Leadership Ideology of Aircraft Commanders. *Journal of Applied Psychology,* 1955, *39,* 82–84.
2. Halpin, A. W. The Leader Behavior and Leadership Ideology of Educational Administrators and Aircraft Commanders. *Harvard Educational Review.* 1955, *25,* 18–32.
3. Halpin, A. W. *The Leadership Behavior of School Superintendents.* Columbus: The Ohio State University, College of Education, 1956.

VI

LEADER BEHAVIOR AND GROUP CHARACTERISTICS

Carl H. Rush, Jr.
Standard Oil Company

There is a school of social theorists which maintains that leadership must be defined in terms of its effects upon the group. Another school maintains that leadership is determined by the group. It is not the purpose of this study to test the merits of either of these claims. This study was designed to determine the relationship between leader behavior and certain characteristics of the group. Two questionnaires were used. The Leader Behavior Description Questionnaire measures two aspects of behavior, Consideration and Initiating Structure. Hemphill's (1) Group Dimensions Description Questionnaire was designed to measure 13 dimensions of groups.

Factor analysis was used to reduce the number of dimensions from 13 to 5. The resulting dimensions are Control, Intimacy, Stratification, Procedural Clarity and Harmony. The names of the factors indicate the group characteristics described by the items which measure the factors. Thus Control is defined as the extent to which the group regulates the behavior of its members while they are functioning as a group. Stratification is the degree to which a group orders its members into status hierarchies.

Three samples of groups and their respective leaders were studied. Sample A consists of 52 air crews which had only recently been assembled. Sample B consists of 70 air crews which had been functioning as crews for a considerable period of time. Sample C consists of 90 crews in combat in Korea. The crews in the three samples were flying B-29 and B-50 bombers. Each crew was described by all members of the crew. In addition, the behavior of the commander of each crew was described by all crew members except the commander himself.

The correlation between the leader behavior scores of the aircraft commanders and the characteristics of the crews are shown in

Table 1. It is seen that Consideration on the part of the leader is correlated with Intimacy and Harmony in the crew. Consideration is correlated negatively with Control and Stratification. Initiating Structure shows a consistently high correlation only with Procedural Clarity.

In all three samples, Consideration scores correlate positively with crew means on the Harmony dimension which suggests that within the complex set of variables which influence the harmony of interpersonal relations, one important variable is the extent to which the aircraft commander (AC) shows consideration for others. It is, of course, impossible to determine from these data whether the air-

TABLE 1—Correlation Between Leader Behavior Dimension Scores and Group Dimension Scores

Group Dimension	Leader Behavior Dimension					
	Consideration			Initiating Structure		
	Sample A	Sample B	Sample C	Sample A	Sample B	Sample C
	r	r	r	r	r	r
Control	—.34[a]	—.14	—.37[b]	—.05	.16	—.12
Intimacy	.25	.33[b]	.40[b]	.08	.09	.32[b]
Harmony	.49[b]	.41[b]	.57[b]	.22	.20	.34[b]
Procedural Clarity	—.06	.30[b]	.19	.52[b]	.41[b]	.41[b]
Stratification	—.47[b]	—.62[b]	—.66[b]	—.22	.01	—.33[b]
Number of Crews	52	70	90	52	70	90

[a] Significant at the .05 level.
[b] Significant at the .01 level.

craft commander is perceived as acting considerately because of the existence of friendly relations in a crew or whether harmony is enhanced by the AC's considerate behavior. In other words, cause and effect relationships cannot be adduced from these correlations. But no matter what the interpretation, the fact remains that these two scores vary concomitantly—more harmonious crews described their AC's as more considerate and vice versa.

It is interesting to note that correlations between Harmony and Initiating Structure tend to be much lower than those between Harmony and Consideration. The actions of the aircraft commander (AC) in setting the structure of crew interaction may be accepted by crew members as a necessary part of the AC's role. As such it has no bearing on, or relationship with, crew harmony. Consideration, on the other hand, is a more personalized or stylistic aspect of the AC's behavior which, because it involves interpersonal contact directly, is seen to be related to Harmony.

The Control dimension shows significant negative correlations with Consideration in samples A and C. In other words, on crews described as having more control the ACs are described as less considerate. Perhaps crew members on these crews perceive the AC as a controlling agent, the personification of institutionalized control.

Intimacy correlates positively with Consideration in Sample B and with both Consideration and Initiating Structure in Sample C. In Sample A these correlations were also positive but less significant. These results seem to add further evidence to the importance of the AC's behavior in setting the psychological atmosphere of the crew. Behaviors which are described as considerate may be influential in establishing a set of relationships such that crew members are able to "get to know each other." On the other hand, perhaps it is only in intimate crews that members know their AC sufficiently well to describe his behavior as considerate. If for example, an AC remains aloof and refuses to become intimate with other crew members, his behavior might be construed as lacking consideration.

Procedural Clarity correlates significantly with Initiating Structure in a positive direction for all three samples. With the exception of Sample B, correlations with Consideration are not significantly different from zero. Here again, the results are quite meaningful in that crew members' descriptions of procedural clarity are positively related to their perceptions of leader behavior in structuring interaction. One of the more important tasks of an AC (or of leaders in general) is to organize the activities of the crew so that each member knows his own role and the roles of others. In a sense the correlations here indicate the success of the AC in such organization, for in those crews which are described as having relatively high Procedural Clarity, the AC is described as initiating a lot of structure. Perhaps the best way to point out the reasonableness of these correlations is to quote part of the definition for the Initiating Structure factor as follows: "High positive loadings on this factor occur on items which imply that the AC organizes and defines the relationship between himself and the members of his crew. He tends to define the role which he expects each member to assume, and endeavors to establish well-defined patterns of organizations, channels of communication, and ways of getting jobs done."

The absence of correlation between Procedural Clarity and Consideration also seems reasonable. Crew members may perceive the structuring as an important part of the AC's job which is reflected in the clarity with which their relationships are established. In this sense there is no value judgment attached to these activities, they are simply things that the leader or AC must do to get the job done. On the other hand, the Consideration factor would seem to have overtones of evaluation or judgment as to the *manner* in which the AC acts. In other words, the methods employed by the AC, whether they be considerate or otherwise, seem to have no relationship with the crew's perception of definition or clarity. What matters is the extent to which the AC sets up this structure and hence facilitates the clarity.

The correlations for Stratification are the highest (Table 1) and show awareness of status differences to be negatively correlated with Consideration. Correlations with Initiating Structure are not significant for Sample A and Sample B but in Sample C there is a significant relationship. These results again suggest the evaluative aspects of the Consideration factor in leader behavior. The "social distance" characteristics of a crew may have important influences on crew members descriptions. If a crew member perceives wide status differences among the crew, with the AC on top so to speak, he is not likely to construe the AC'c behavior as considerate. Thus the negative correlations between these two factors become reasonable. To expect anything else would be disregarding the influence of status perceptions in the description of behavior.

A possible interpretation of this influence has been advanced in terms of the AC's "respect" for other crew members. One distinction between egalitarian and authoritarian leaders may be made in terms of respect for the opinions, actions, and feelings of other group members. Thus the same physical actions of two leaders may be perceived differently on the basis of sincerity or respect. Condescension would seem to characterize the behavior of authoritarian leaders and this attitude is likely to be perceived by the recipients. Thus the AC who rides the crest of a heightened status system may "make sounds" like a considerate leader but because of the condescension or lack of respect, crew members will not perceive these actions as considerate. Perhaps this would account for the strong negative relationships between Stratification and Consideration.

Summarizing the correlations between group dimensions and the two dimensions of leader behavior, it would seem that results are consistent with expectations. There is a danger of course in inferring the reasonableness of these results because of the "naming" process in the factor analysis. One must guard against reading into factor designations more than was in the basic data and this problem is especially crucial when a set of such factors is interrelated. However, exercise of caution in the interpretation of results in this section still points to a meaningful set of relationships between ascribed crew characteristics and descriptions of leader behavior.

References

1. Hemphill, John K. *Group Dimensions: A Manual for Their Measurement.* Columbus: The Ohio State University, Bureau of Business Research Monograph No. 87, 1956.

VII

LEADER BEHAVIOR ASSOCIATED WITH THE ADMINISTRATIVE REPUTATIONS OF COLLEGE DEPARTMENTS[1]

John K. Hemphill
Educational Testing Service

This paper reports the results of a study of leadership and administration in 22 departments in the Liberal Arts College of a moderately large university. The study was designed to explore the relationship between the leader behavior of the departmental administrator and the reputation of his department for being well administered. It also sought to determine the usefulness of reputational data as criteria of administrative quality.

Methods

Cooperation of the dean of the Liberal Arts College and the 22 department heads was secured at the outset of the study. Later all faculty members were acquainted with the nature and objectives of the study by means of (a) a letter of introduction signed by the dean, (b) personal meetings with each department's faculty, and (c) written instructions relative to completing a packet of anonymous questionnaires. Although participation was voluntary, 234 of the 322 faculty members returned their questionnaires after two follow-up letters.

The following questionnaires were administered[2] to the 22 department chairmen, and to the faculty members of the 22 departments: a Background Information Questionnaire, the Leader Behavior Description Questionnaire, the Group Dimensions Questionnaire, and a Reputational Ranking form. Each of the questionnaires is described briefly below.

---

[1] This study is reprinted by permsision of the *Journal of Educational Psychology*.
[2] The data for this study were collected by Mr. Vernon J. Bentz, who also participated in the planning of the research.

Background Information Questionnaire: This form secured data concerning the respondent's department affiliation, age, sex, academic rank, degree held, length of time in his department, length of association as a member of an academic faculty, publications, affiliation with other professional organizations and job satisfaction.

The Leader Behavior Description Questionnaire: The form used in this study consisted of 150 items; however, only 30 of this number were actually scored. This decision resulted from extensive factor analyses of all the items. Two scores are obtained: (a) Consideration and (b) Initiating Structure. *Consideration* refers to behavior on the part of a leader that is characterized by warm friendly relations with group members, concern with group member welfare, respect for their integrity, etc. *Initiating Structure* refers to activities on the part of a leader that introduce organization, new ways of doing things, and new procedures for solving group problems, etc. The 22 department chairmen described their own behavior. Their behavior was also described by the faculty members of their departments: one third of the members selected at random from each department used the questionnaire to describe both the *actual* and the *ideal* behavior of the chairmen of their departments.

The Group Dimension Questionnaire: The development of this questionnaire is described in detail by Hemphill (1). It yields scores on 13 dimensions or characteristics of groups. The respondents (faculty members) described their departments by indicating how well the items assigned to each dimension characterize their respective departments as groups.

The definitions of the dimensions and the number of items in each are listed below.

1. *Autonomy* is the degree to which a group functions independently of other groups and occupies an independent position in society (13 items).

2. *Control* is the degree to which a group regulates the behavior of individuals while they are functioning as group members (12 items).

3. *Flexibility* is the degree to which a group's activities are marked by informal procedures rather than by adherence to established procedures (13 items).

4. *Hedonic Tone* is the degree to which group membership is accompanied by a general feeling of pleasantness or agreeableness (5 items).

5. *Homogeneity* is the degree to which members of a group are similar in socially relevant characteristics (15 items).

6. *Intimacy* is the degree to which members of a group are mutually acquainted with one another and are familiar with the more personal details of one another's lives (13 items).

7. *Participation* is the degree to which members of a group apply equal effort to group activities (10 items).

8. *Permeability* is the degree to which a group permits ready access to membership (13 items).

9. *Polarization* is the degree to which a group is oriented and works toward a single goal which is clear and specific to all members (12 items).

10. *Potency* is the degree to which a group has primary significance for its members (15 items).

11. *Stability* is the degree to which the group resists changes in its size and in turnover of its members (5 items).

12. *Stratification* is the degree to which a group orders its members into status hierarchies (12 items).

13. *Viscidity* is the degree to which members of the group function as a unit (15 items).

The Reputational Ranking Form: This form is based on the methodology of the "nominating technique." The form was prefaced with these directions:

> "it is desirable to ascertain an estimate of departmental 'reputation.' *Not including your own department*, rank the five departments in the Liberal Arts College that have general reputations on the campus for being 'Best Led' or 'Best Administered' departments.
>
> "You are not asked to give your own personal evaluation, but asked to give the general reputation of the department, using as your point of reference what 'most people in the College of Liberal Arts would agree' that a given department has as a given reputation. For example, you may personally think a certain department is poorly led but know that the reputation of that department on the campus is generally higher than your own personal opinion would rate it. In making the ranking use this general campus reputation."

Similar instructions also were given with a request for the five departments that were reputed to be "Least Well Lead" or "Less Well Administered." With completion of the form the respondent had indicated his knowledge of the campus reputation of 10 departments and by implication had placed the 12 remaining departments in a category not distinguished by reputations of being either well administered or poorly administered.

Analysis of Data

The analysis of data was planned in a manner to provide tentative answers to many questions that are raised when reputational information is suggested as a criterion of quality of administration. Among these questions are:

1. Is there any degree of consistency or agreement among the individuals who report knowledge of reputations of the different departments?
2. Are these reputational rankings made by individuals qualified to know existing campus opinions?
3. What characteristics of a department or of the behavior of its chairman are reflected in the department's campus reputation with respect to quality of administration?

Scoring of the Reputational Rankings

A relatively arbitrary scoring procedure was adopted for the purpose of summarizing the data secured by the reputational ranking forms. Weights were assigned each nomination received by a department according to the following scheme:

Nomination	Weight
First Best Administered	5
Second Best Administered	4
Third Best Administered	3
Fourth Best Administered	2
Fifth Best Administered	1
First Less Well Administered	—5
Second Less Well Administered	—4
Third Less Well Administered	—3
Fourth Less Well Administered	—2
Fifth Less Well Administered	—1
Not nominated for either category	0

A score was derived for each department, being the sum of the weights assigned to the nominations that were received. Scores ranged from 271 to 305.

Results

The presentation of the results of the analysis of the data will be organized about the three major questions that were asked concerning the characteristics of "reputation for being well administered" as a criterion of administrative effectiveness.

What is the degree of consistency or agreement among the reputations reported for the various departments?—This question was answered by establishing two samples of respondents and determining the agreement between the two sets of reputation scores derived

TABLE 1—Average Scores on Consideration and Initiating Structure of Department Chairmen as Described by the Department Members

Department	Consideration		Initiating Structure	
	Ideal	Actual	Ideal	Actual
	Mean	Mean	Mean	Mean
A[a]	44.00	45.33	44.67	42.67
B	51.00	42.00	46.50	30.67
C[a]	49.33	48.10	45.50	43.50
D	43.00	24.33	34.33	33.00
E[a]	46.38	42.06	36.92	36.65
F	45.50	38.25	44.75	44.50
G[a]	53.00	35.00	50.00	26.50
I[a]	47.75	49.60	41.75	49.20
J	45.50	49.50	42.00	25.50
K[a]	47.29	41.14	38.43	38.86
L	47.33	40.00	42.67	32.50
N[a]	49.00	44.75	39.63	37.75
O	49.25	43.67	47.00	44.33
Q[a]	48.00	47.00	36.25	39.00
R	50.25	38.33	40.75	34.00
S	50.00	34.00	40.50	25.00
T[a]	46.55	49.22	39.66	40.22
U	51.00	43.20	38.75	35.80

[a] These departments were above the median on "reputation."

from the two samples. The two samples of respondents include only those who made relatively complete nominations (8, 9 or 10, of the 5 best administered and the 5 less well administered) and was constituted so as to have an approximately equal number of respondents in both samples from the different departments. Table 1 shows the "reputation scores" of the department as derived from the two samples. The correlation between the two sets (Sample A vs. Sample B) of "reputations" scores is .935. If Spearman-Brown's correction is applied to this coefficient the reliability of these reputation scores becomes .97.

We can have considerable confidence in the existence of a campus reputation with respect to quality of departmental administration. It also is apparent that this reputation is known and can be reported with a high degree of agreement among members of the college faculty.

What are the characteristics of those faculty members who completed the Reputational Ranking Form?—Not all of the faculty members who cooperated in the study by returning questionnaires completed the Reputational Ranking Form. Many faculty members indicated on the face of the form that they were unaware of campus opinion regarding administrative reputation of departments. Others made only a portion of the 10 nominations requested. It was possible to establish two groups of respondents on the basis of their response to the Reputational Ranking Form. Group I consisted of 73 faculty members who provided at least 8 of the 10 nominations requested. Group II consisted of 101 faculty members who completed the other questionnaires composing their packets but failed to make a single nomination on the Reputational Ranking Form. A comparison of data available concerning characteristics of these two groups of respondents indicated that those faculty members who provided nominations were considerably older, and (what perhaps is more important) had been members of the faculty longer. For example, 51 per cent of the respondents who returned completed forms were more than 50 years of age; only 24 per cent of those who returned blank forms had reached the age of 50 years. Of the respondents who returned completed forms, 60 per cent had been members of the faculty 6 years or longer. This compares with 25 per cent of the respondents who returned blank forms.

It is to be expected that campus reputations of college departments are known through long associations of faculty members. Individuals who are relatively "new" on the campus are likely to be unaware of events significant in establishing a department's reputation for administrative excellence. We interpret the tendency of the more mature and longer experienced faculty members to complete this form to be indicative of validity of the information obtained. We also must accept the fact that judging campus reputation of departments may be a meaningless and impossible task for a large portion of the younger faculty.

Is the reputation of departments for being well administered related to the style of the department chairman's leadership?—The packets of questionnaires that were distributed to the members of each department included the Leader Behavior Description Questionnaire, General Form. One third of the members of each department completed this questionnaire to provide their descriptions of the leadership behavior of the chairman of their respective departments. Another third of the members of each department completed this same questionnaire but indicated what an "ideal" chairman for their department should do. For 18 of the 22 departments descriptions were available of the actual behavior of their chairman from at least 2 and as many as 17 department members. For each of these 18 departments, an average Consideration score and an average Initiating Structure score was calculated. For each of these 18 departments an "ideal" norm was also computed by averaging scores on Consideration and Initiating Structure from the information supplied by department members who completed the questionnaires to provide this information. Table 1 presents the average scores for both "actual" and "ideal" leadership behavior.

Pearson product moment correlation coefficients were computed to express the relationship between each of the two dimensions of actual leadership behavior and the "reputation" score of the departments. Correlations were also computed to express the relationship between the absolute discrepancy (either positive or negative) between "actual" and "ideal" leadership behavior on the two dimensions. These data are presented in Table 2.

TABLE 2—Correlation Coefficients Expressing the Relationship Between the Administrative "Reputation" Scores of 18 College Departments and Four Leadership Scores of the Department Chairmen As Described by Department Members

Score	Mean	S D	Correlation with Reputation Score
Reputation	21.7	133.8	—
"Actual" Consideration	42.2	6.4	.36
Discrepancy between "Actual" and "Ideal" Consideration	—6.9	5.6	—.52[a]
"Actual" Initiating Structure	36.8	6.7	.48[a]
Discrepancy between "Actual" and "Ideal" Initiating Structure	—6.3	6.9	—.55[a]

[a] A correlation coefficient of .47 is significant at the .05 level.

By reference to Table 2 it can be seen that there is some relationship between the style of leadership of the department chairman as this is viewed by department members and the department reputation on the campus for being well or poorly administered. This is especially true if we view the actual behavior of the department chairman from what is held to be "ideal" behavior by members of his department. Departments that achieve a reputation for good administration are those led by chairmen who attend to both of the facets of leadership measured in this study, i.e., they concern themselves with (1) organizing departmental activities and initiating new ways of solving department problems, and (2) at the same time develop warm considerate relationship with members of the department.

If we examine the leadership patterns of department chairmen closely we note a conjunctive relationship between Consideration and Initiating Structure suggesting that minimal amount of both behaviors is required for achievement of good reputation, and that an excess of one type of behavior does not compensate for the lack of the other. An excess of Consideration behavior can not compensate for a deficiency in Initiating Structure and vice versa. If a multiple cutting score of 41 on Consideration and 36 on Initiating Structure were utilized, the reputation of the department in terms of being above or below the median could have been successfully identified in 16 out of 18 cases. The data for this comparison are given in Table 3.

TABLE 3—The Relationship Between the "Reputation" Achieved by College Departments and the Consideration and Initiating Structure Scores of 18 Department Chairmen

Chairman's Leadership	Reputation of Department	
	Above Median	Below Median
Score of 41 or larger on Consideration *and* a score of 36 or more on Initiating Structure	Departments: A C E I K N Q T	Department: 0
Score of less than 41 on Consideration *or* a score of less than 36 on Initiating Structure	Department: F	Departments: D G J L R S U

The x^2 value computed for the data in Table 3 is 8.00, significant beyond the .01 level of confidence.

A further means of examining the conjunctive relation between these two facets of leadership behavior is available from the discrepancies score. The total of the two discrepancy scores of department chairmen correlates .63 (.01 level of confidence) with the reputation scores. This result suggests that department chairmen must meet the expectations of their faculties with respect to both Consideration and Initiating Structure if the department is to achieve a favorable reputation on the campus. In the remainder of the presentation of results we shall examine various other characteristics of the departments for relationship with their administrative "reputation."

TABLE 4—Correlation Between Each of Thirteen Group Dimensions (Average Scores) and Departments' "Reputation" for Being Well Administered (N = 18)

Reputation Correlated with:	Mean	S D	r[a]
Autonomy	34.39	4.02	.09
Control	28.67	3.35	—.07
Flexibility	37.61	5.83	.02
Hedonic Tone	18.78	2.10	.16
Homogeniety	33.06	3.70	—.05
Intimacy	48.39	4.39	—.02
Participation	46.36	4.53	.29
Permeability	22.50	4.30	—.04
Polarization	38.39	5.62	.05
Potency	51.06	4.59	.05
Stability	15.06	2.76	—.06
Stratification	40.72	5.09	.05
Viscidity	35.50	8.15	.04

[a] r = .47 is significant at the .05 level.

Are the characteristics of their department as seen by department members related to the "reputation" of their department?—The Group Dimensions Questionnaire was distributed to two thirds of each department's members. The questionnaire provides a score on each of 13 group characteristics. This score was calculated as the average of the descriptions supplied by those department members who completed this questionnaire. Average scores based on a minimum of two member's descriptions were available for 18 of the 22 departments. Pearson correlation coefficients were computed for each of the 13 dimensions and the "reputation" score. The correlations are shown in Table 4.

None of the correlations reported in Table 4 is statistically significant. There appears to be no relationship between the manner in which department members characterized their respective departments by use of the Group Description Questionnaire and the "reputation" of the departments for being well administered. The only suggestions of such possible relationships involve Participation and Hedonic Tone. If these small and not statistically significant relationships could be shown to exist with further study, departments with reputation for good administration may also be those in which faculty members feel they can participate in department activities, and hence find them more pleasant departments in which to have membership. However, the important finding is the lack of significant relationship between the faculty member's general impression of various characteristics of their departments and the campus reputation of the department's administration. In a sense this lack of relationship makes the earlier reported finding of relationship between the behavior of the department chairman and administrative reputation more significant. It points, also, to chairman behavior specifically, rather than to a general impression about the department, as the more likely determiner of "reputation."

Are there relationships between "demographic" characteristics of departments and their "reputation?"—Examination was made of each of the following "Demographic" characteristics of the 22 departments and their "reputation" scores:

1. Age of faculty members (Average)
2. Size of the department (Number of members)
3. Length of service to the department of its faculty members (Average number of years)
4. Length of academic experience of each department faculty (Average number of years)
5. Academic rank of members (Per cent Associate Professors, or Professors)
6. Educational attainment of faculty of the departments (Per cent with Ph.D)
7. Publications record of department members. (Index based on number and "quality" of publications)

Only one of these 7 "demographic" variables showed a relationship with reputation. It was found that large departments tended to receive higher reputation scores (r between number of members and reputation $= .58$, significant at the .05 level). Two hypotheses were advanced in an effort to account for this relation. *First,* it was suggested that larger departments might require more Initiating Structure behavior on the part of the chairmen, and since Initiating Structure has been shown to be related to "reputation," the relationship to department "size" could be a function of the same underlying variables. The *second* explanation involved the suggestion that the significance of administration in large (compared with smaller) departments is well recognized by deans and other central officials of the college administration, and that in selecting department heads for larger departments more care had been exercised. In other words, in the cases of very small departments, chairmen might be appointed on the basis of seniority with little regard for other qualifications, but in large departments demonstrated ability to assume administrative responsibility would be a prerequisite to appointment.

The first of the two hypotheses could be checked in part by determining the relation between the size of the department and the Initiating Structure behavior of their chairmen. This correlation was computed and found to be .11 which is not significant. The available evidence favors the second interpretation.

Summary

Campus reputations of 22 college departments for being well administered were secured from members of the faculty of a Liberal Arts College. As parts of the same research study data were also secured concerning: (a) the leadership behavior of department chairmen as viewed and as wanted by department members, (b) group characteristics of departments as viewed by department members, and (c) demographic characteristics of the departments. An examination was made of the relationships among these data in an effort to assess the usefulness of campus opinion as a criterion of quality of administration. The following conclusions resulted from the analysis:

1. Administrative "reputation" of the college department was reliably reported by faculty members. Agreement between two independent samples of respondents was very high ($r = .94$).
2. Older and more mature faculty members provided a larger proportion of the "reputation" information than "younger" or "new" members of the faculty.
3. "Reputation" for being well administered is related to the leadership

behavior of department chairmen as this behavior is described by department members. Those departments with best "reputations" for good administration have chairmen who are described as above the average on *both* Consideration and Initiating Structure and as more nearly meeting the behavior expected of an ideal chairman.
4. Larger departments tend to have better administrative reputations than smaller departments. This fact is independent of the Initiating Structure activity of the chairman and may indicate only that more care is exercised in selecting chairmen of large departments.
5. With the exception of size, all group characteristics of the departments, both demographic characteristics and those described by means of the Group Description Questionnaire, showed no significant relationship to reputation for good administration.

References

1. Hemphill, John K. *Group Dimensions: A Manual for Their Measurement.* Columbus: Ohio State University, Bureau of Business Research Monograph No. 87, 1956.

VIII

A COMPARISON OF GENERAL AND SPECIFIC LEADER BEHAVIOR DESCRIPTIONS

MELVIN SEEMAN

The Ohio State University

One of the recurring problems in the study of leadership, as this volume itself attests, is that of achieving an objective portrait of how the leader behaves—a portrait that discriminates among presumed differences in leadership style and is reasonably free of halo effect. The halo problem is, of course, not unique to leadership research; but in light of American norms and stereotypes about leadership, the halo question is especially difficult when we are attempting to describe the behavior of leaders. Myrdal, (7) for example, has argued that the idea of leadership is more omnipresent in American culture than in most European societies. He notes that, for all our egalitarian emphasis, "the idea of leadership pervades American thought and collective action," though, on the other hand, "Americans are in general quite unaware that the leadership idea is a particular characteristic of their culture," and "regularly show a marked reluctance to admit the fact even when it is pointed out by the observer."

Given such a pervasive, yet rationally unexamined, stress upon leadership, one might expect serious difficulties in achieving an objective description of a given leader's behavior. The leader's performance, especially in American culture, is presumably heavily laden with both positive and negative affect; and it becomes imperative that we examine carefully the variety of tools designed to yield descriptions of this socially-charged behavior.

The purpose of this paper is to make a contribution to this comparative task, by examining the results obtained when two different sets of scales for measuring leader behavior are applied to a common set of organizational leaders. Unfortunately, the number of respondents (as well as the number of leaders) is smaller than one would prefer; but we may provide, at the least, some basis for gauging what our hopes and cautions might appropriately be when we describe the behavior of leaders in given ways.

PLAN OF THE STUDY

Our data were obtained as part of a larger project aimed at examining leadership style among school executives. The larger study reviewed the performance of some 75 school leaders in 26 Ohio communities; and its purpose was to show how leadership style within the schools is a function of community and cultural pressures surrounding the organization (10). In 12 of these 26 communities, two different forms for the description of the superintendent's leadership were distributed. One of these, which we shall call the "General Form" was the Leader Behavior Description Questionnaire (LBDQ), consisting at the time of 150 items to which the respondent applied a five-point frequency scale. It was from these items that the factor scores titled "Consideration" and "Initiating Structure" were developed by Halpin and Winer; and in our scoring we have used only the relevant items for these two measures. In each case, the score was based upon responses to 15 items. The items thus selected are labeled the "General Form" because they do not specify the institutionally-relevant content of behavior, and can thus be used to describe the leader of almost any group. Thus, for example, one of the "Initiating Structure" items asserts, "He tries out his new ideas in the group," while one of the "Consideration" items reads, "He does little things to make it pleasant to be a member of the group." The content of his "new ideas" and of the "little things" are unspecified, and the respondent simply indicates how often the leader in question performs as indicated.

The second type of leadership description we have called the "Specific Scales," since they were developed especially for use in a school setting. The scales were designed to measure four aspects of the school leader's behavior. Though it is unnecessary to reproduce the full list of items, it would be helpful for our comparison of the two types of scales to indicate what the four aspects were, and to illustrate the contextual character of the items by presenting one item from each scale. The ideal definitions of the four specific leader behavior measures, and the sample items are given below (all items being scored on a 7-point scale):

Leader Behavior Measures

1. *Communication:* the extent to which there is expression (either upward or downward) of ideas, notices, attitudes, information, or rules relating to the operation of the organization.
2. *Separatism:* The extent to which the leader interacts formally with group members; insists on being recognized as occupying a clearly unique and different position with respect to other members rather than functioning as just another member of the group.
3. *Change:* the extent to which the leader is receptive to change in the organization; initiates change himself or facilitates change; rewards subordinate behavior which is non-conforming to established custom or procedure.
4. *Domination:* the extent to which the leader restricts the group's decision-making power; does not permit individual freedom on the job; suppresses individual expression.

Sample Items

1. How often have you gone to see the leader on your own initiative to talk over a problem on the job? (Scored, "Very often" to "Never")
2. Has your leader tended to take an active part in routine or extra-curricular school activities—such as working on committees for special events; participation in club work; or planning for school parties? (Scored, "Very characteristic of him" to "Not at all characteristic")
3. What sort of reaction have you received when talking with the leader about new methods you tried out in the classroom? (Scored, "Very definite interest or encouragement" to "Practically no interest or encouragement")
4. In cases where a student's passing or failing is doubtful, does the leader leave the decision pretty much up to you? (Scored, "Always" to "Never")

The construction and pre-testing of the items for the four specific scales are described elsewhere (8). The final version of these scales (as used in this study) included the following number of items in each behavior dimension: communication, 12; separatism, 10; change, 8; and domination, 11. Generality and specificity are, of course, relative matters; and our intention was to construct a series of scales which would tap the more important specific relationships between leader and subordinate in the school situation, while retaining the possibility that the particular content of each item might be readily converted for comparative use in other kinds of organizations (e.g. in business or in military).

We distributed the LBDQ in 12 communities where the complement of elementary school teachers was large enough to warrant distribution of both leader behavior forms. The LBDQ forms were randomly interspersed with the specific forms. A total of 71 usable LBDQ responses was received; and in 9 of the 12 communities there were at least 4 describers of the same school superintendent. From the larger group of respondents using the specific scales in these same communities, we selected a sample of teachers whose background characteristics (age and years of teaching experience, for example) matched those of the respondents using the LBDQ. The final matched samples of 71 teachers using the LBDQ and 71 teachers using the specific description, were composed in both cases of 62 females and 9 males. The degree to which the two samples were

TABLE 1—Background Characteristics of Matched Samples Using General and Specific Leader Behavior Description Scales

Variable	General Sample		Specific Sample	
	Mean	S.D.	Mean	S.D.
Age	3.49	2.03	3.63	2.07
Salary	4.41	2.17	4.35	1.84
Years Teaching Experience	5.23	2.29	4.87	2.65
Length of Time in Present School System	4.18	2.82	3.94	2.71
Years Served Under Current School Leader	3.17	2.63	3.06	2.72
Degree of Job Satisfaction	6.00	1.08	5.87	1.17

successfully matched on other relevant variables is indicated in Table 1, which presents (in terms of coded IBM scores) the means and standard deviations for the matched samples on six personal history variables. The evidence in Table 1 indicates that the two samples are highly comparable on these six measures, both in mean level and in the dispersion of scores as indicated by the standard deviations. None of the differences between samples is statistically significant.

Another way to view the comparability of the two samples is provided by their respective scores on 6 additional measures. For purposes of the larger study, we asked each teacher to provide the following ratings:

1. *Evaluation*: a rating of the superintendent's effectiveness as a school leader, using a 9- item, 7-point scale.

2. *Leader Status*: a rating (based upon 18 items) of the community status level of the leader, where status is defined as placement in terms of social, economic, prestige and influence rank.

3. *Teacher Status*: a rating of the teacher's status in the community on these same four hierarchies of rank.

4. *Status Difference*: an index of the perceived difference in status between teacher and leader (derived from a comparison of the scores assigned in 2 and 3 above).

5. *Ambivalence*: an index of the degree of difficulty the teacher experienced in choosing between two forced-choice alternatives, on 12 items which contrasted a relatively directive as against a nondirective leadership style.

6. *Status Attitude*: a measure of the generalized attitudes about status held by the individual—i.e. the extent to which the individual can be characterized as generally equalitarian (against the preservation of status differences) or nonequalitarian.

The reliability of these six measures, and their substantive relation to the problem of leadership, are described in full elsewhere (10). Here we are simply interested in noting that, though our matching was accomplished on the basis of similarity on the background variables presented in Table 1, the two samples show a high degree of comparability as well on these "attitude" measures which were not directly involved in the matching process. Table 2 presents

TABLE 2—Comparison, on Six Rating Scale Measures, of Matched Samples Using General and Specific Leader Behavior Description Scales

Variable	General Sample		Specific Sample	
	Mean	S.D.	Mean	S.D.
Evaluation	4.49	2.35	4.58	1.99
Leader Status	5.92	1.55	5.51	1.65
Teacher Status	4.99	1.92	4.52	2.04
Status Difference	4.85	1.51	4.83	1.86
Ambivalence	3.30	2.29	3.32	2.12
Status Attitude	4.86	1.85	4.52	1.57

the data comparing the general sample and the specific sample on these six measures; and it is clear that the correspondence is close indeed. Again, none of the differences in Table 2 is statistically significant.

THE RELIABILITY OF THE SCALES

Given the presumption, on the basis of this evidence, that we are dealing with two reasonably comparable samples of teachers describing the behavior of a common group of superintendents, we may proceed to observe how the two types of scales perform. The first question of interest concerns the relative reliability of the two kinds of measures. For the total group of 71 teachers using the general scales, the corrected split-half reliabilities of the consideration and initiating structure scores were .89 and .87, respectively. For the four specific leader behavior scales, the corrected reliabilities were: communication, .79; separatism, .87; change, .88; and domination, .77. Thus, two of the specific scales approximate the same reliability figure as the general scales, while two of them are appreciably lower in reliability, though still satisfactory for group use. For both sets of scales, evidence from other studies indicates that these reliability figures are typical. In a pilot study using the specific scales, a quite comparable set of reliability figures was obtained. Halpin reports split-half reliabilities of .83 and .92 for initiating structure and consideration, respectively (3).

One may surmise from this evidence that though there is no sharp difference between the two types of scales in their performance with regard to reliability, the likelihood is that the general scales will tend to yield somewhat higher reliabilities. We must remember, however, as both Campbell (1) and Hammond (5) have suggested in discussing the use of indirect measures of social attitudes, that high reliabilities may reflect not so much the consistency of the behavior being described but the strain toward consistency of the respondent himself. As Campbell (1) has put it,

> "...it should be noted that direct tests uniformly have much higher reliability coefficients than do indirect ones, especially when the number of items and time of administration are considered. Of course this consistency is in part conscious, voluntary and possibly superficial —in contrast to the involuntary 'bias' in performance achieved by many indirect tests."

We are pointing here to the possibility that the description of leader behavior through the use of general items may increase respondent consistency at the cost of accuracy in description—that is, to the extent that the items do not direct the respondent's attention to fairly specific behavior to be described, he may build into his responses a consistency which reflects his own needs or attitudes more than it reflects the consistency of the leader's behavior. We shall return to this point in the next section, but here we should note that the specific scales, too, have their own difficulties. One of these is that the most appropriate degree of specificity is not easy to determine: one may, as Wherry's work suggests (11), easily become so specific that the items no longer have any real applicability to the population being described, and both reliability and discriminating power are consequently seriously reduced.

THE DIMENSION INTERCORRELATIONS

This discussion takes us quite naturally to the question of the degree of intercorrelation which holds within the two types of scales. For the general form, the correlation in our sample between consideration and initiating structure was .28. The intercorrelations of the four specific scales for our comparable group of 71 teachers, are given in Table 3. The average r in Table 3, without regard to sign is .46.

TABLE 3—Intercorrelation Among Four Specific Leader Behavior Description Scales (N = 71)

Leader Behavior Description	Leader Behavior Description			
	Communication	Separation	Change	Domination
	r	r	r	r
Communication		—.38	.40	—.38
Separation	—.38		—.60	.56
Change	.40	—.60		—.49
Domination	—.38	.56	—.49	

These results are rather consistent with those obtained in other studies. Halpin, for example, reports a correlation of .18 between the two general dimensions for a sample of 50 educational administrators whose leadership was decried by teachers. These correlations (in the present study and in Halpin's work) between initiating structure and consideration are gratifyingly low, since we presumably wish to use measures of leadership style which are relatively independent of each other. But other evidence indicates that, as we might expect, variation in either the type of describer or the institutional situation can make a significant difference in the association between the scales. Thus, for example, Fleischman found a correlation as high as .56 between the two dimensions when the general scales were used by industrial foremen to describe their supervisors' behavior, and he found it necessary to reassess the factors originally obtained with an Air Force sample. Fleischman (2) comments:

> "The foremen may have responded to certain items in each key according to their judgment of 'What a good leader is,' instead of simply describing their own superior's behavior. This is the 'halo effect' so common to instruments of this type; the more 'halo,' the higher the correlation between dimension scores."

Halpin (3) has reported a correlation of .45 for these two dimensions in a military situation, and he notes that when school board members, rather than teachers, described the leader (for the same group of superintendents where the .18 correlation was obtained for teacher descriptions) a correlation of .61 between initiating structure and consideration was found. Halpin's (4) comment on this finding goes as follows:

> "The fact that the board description interdimension correlation is higher than the corresponding correlation for staff descriptions suggests that the superintendents can stress both dimensions of behavior when they believe that this is sufficiently worth the effort—especially in dealing with members of the board.... The present findings indicate that the superintendents differentiate their role behavior. In dealing with their boards they tend to be effective as leaders, but they are inclined to be less effective in working with their staffs."

There is a good deal of credibility in this view; but it is also credible to believe that these results tell us as much about the describing groups as they do about the behavior of the superintendents in question. The point is that school board members, who hire and fire and are responsible for the leader they are describing may well need to see them as more clearly effective—which here means high in both initiating structure and consideration; and it may well be that general scales, which do not specify the behavior they are to describe, maximize the opportunity for them to subjectivize their report. In the final analysis, it is impossible to say how much realism and how much distortion is contained in the clearly different report, in Halpin's study, by the board members as against the teachers.

We are inclined to the view that this evidence on scale intercorrelations raises some doubts regarding both types of scales. For the general scale, it seems clear that one of its major virtues—namely, easy applicability to a broad range of situations—is brought into question by the relatively high r's which have been obtained between the two dimensions in military, industrial and educational situations (these high r's necessitating, in some instances, revision of the scales before they become maximably useful). The specific scales, on the other hand, are no better in this regard. On the whole, their dimension intercorrelations are probably somewhat higher, and it remains a question whether these r's could be significantly and consistently reduced through further refinement. What we presumably need (and this need is indicated by some of the data to be presented later as well) is a set of studies, using both general and specific scales, where there is an opportunity to derive an objective, observational record of leader behavior against which the scale responses can be compared. Thus, we seem, at present, to be in about the following situation:

1. The general scales, in our sample, yield low dimension intercorrelation (and this is consistent with the descriptions by teachers in Halpin's studies).

2. The specific scales yield dimension intercorrelations which, though somewhat higher, are low enough generally speaking to permit a good deal of independent variation among the several scores.

3. In the absence of behavioral observations of leadership style, it seems that we choose, when we elect to use one set of scales as against the other, between a somewhat "cleaner" description of two generalized aspects of leadership style and a somewhat more "contaminated" set of scores which attempt to make finer distinctions among leadership styles. Observational studies may aid in telling us how "clean" and how "contaminated" (and under what conditions) the two types of reports may be.

We are well aware of the fact that *any* report through scales or direct observation by participants or outsiders is an abstraction mediated by the observer's frame of reference, and we are not seeking for an "ultimately real" portrait of the leader's behavior. But we are not forced, on this account, to accept the view that any report is valid simply because it is reported, or is equally valid in comparison with other observers' reports. To be sure, the teachers (or the board members) report what they do; and this report is of intrinsic interest and is useful for certain purposes. But we are obligated then to investigate why they report as they do, or the nature of the discrepancies in various reports. We "triangulate," so to speak, all our observations upon the event in the effort to understand it, and in the process inevitably make interpretations of the congruence or disagreement among observers. In ths sense, it is not enough to insist that each observation point is equally valid and thus retreat to the position "to each his own."

THE RELATION OF LEADERSHIP TO OTHER VARIABLES

We examine next whether the two types of scales are significantly different as far as their association with other variables is concerned. We have, in effect, three types of variables here: first, there are the objective personal history variables (i.e., length of time the individual has been in the given school system; length of service with the leader in question; salary; age; and years of teaching experience); second, there are the "directly job-related" attitudes (i.e., evaluation of the leader; a rating on personal job satisfaction; and a description of personal ambivalence about ideal leadership choices); and third, there are the status measures (i.e., a rating of the leader's status position; the teacher's status position; the status difference between them; and an index of status attitudes). The correlation of each of these variables with the general and specific leadership scores is given in Table 4.

The outcomes presented in Table 4 can be summarized as follows:

1. As far as the personal history variables are concerned, both sets of scales are reasonably free of major influence; and this is presumably all to the good if we assume that the behavior of the leader is in fact reasonably constant for all staff members. The only statistically significant trend is that "old-hands" (as defined either in terms of years of experience, length of time in the system, or number of years served under the present leader) tend to report *less* initiating structure and *more* domination.

2. The "job-related attitudes," as one might expect, show the

TABLE 4—Correlations Between Two Types of Leader Behavior Description Scales and Three Types of Self-Report Variables (N = 71)

Self-Report Variable	"General" Scales		"Specific" Scales			
	Initiating Structure	Considera- tion	Commu- cation	Separat- ism	Change	Domina- tion
	r	r	r	r	r	r
Personal History						
Age	—.13	—.20	—.08	.17	—.18	.16
Salary	.10	—.08	.02	.22	—.18	.21
Years Teaching Experience	—.39[b]	—.06	.01	.17	—.13	.26[a]
Length of Time in Present School System	—.11	—.02	.02	.14	—.15	.25[a]
Years Served Under Present School Leader	—.34[b]	—.17	.23	.18	—.20	.09
Job-Related Attitudes						
Evaluation of Leader	.36[b]	.68[b]	.44[b]	—.54[b]	.67[b]	—.67[b]
Personal Job Satisfaction	.09	.21	.09	—.32[b]	.49[b]	—.46[b]
Ambivalence	.21	.02	.01	—.08	.06	.01
Status Measures						
Leader Status	.22	.33[b]	.31[b]	—.23	.54[b]	—.29[a]
Teacher Status	.12	.30[a]	.31[b]	—.30[a]	.30[a]	—.35[b]
Status Difference	.10	.06	.10	.00	.28[a]	—.05
Status Attitude	.00	.03	—.30[a]	.00	.02	.01

[a] Significant at the .05 level of confidence.
[b] Significant at the .01 level of confidence.

highest and most consistent relationship to leadership description; and this is more true for the specific than for the general scales. For all six leadership measures (the two general scores and the four specific ones) the evaluation of the leader is significantly related to the reported leadership style. Most of these r's are reasonably high for both types of scales, and the pattern is as one would expect: high consideration and high evaluation of the leader go together (.68); while for the specific scales the preferred pattern is constituted by high communication, low separatism, high change, and low domination. Again, it is interesting to note that the r's for initiating structure and for domination are reversed: high evaluation goes with *high* initiating structure, but with *low* domination.

3. The ratings of status position are also significantly related to leadership description; and this is more consistently true for the specific scales as compared with the two general scales.

On the whole, the evidence in Table 4 does not argue very well for the notion that specific scales will significantly reduce the degree of halo involved in the description of leadership; and, if anything, the reverse seems to be the case. The individual's "job satisfaction," for example, is more consistently and significantly reflected in his description of the leader on the specific scales than on the general ones; and to some extent the results with the status measures argue in the same direction. One intriguing fact which these data point up is that initiating structure and domination are concepts which lie in different planes, so to speak, since it is consistently true that the relationships for these two measures are not parallel but reversed.

The Discrimination Among Leadership Styles—All of the material reported above deals with our total of 71 matched cases. As noted earlier, there were 9 communities in which we had a minimum of 4 describers for the same superintendent, involving a total sample of 63 matched cases. If we assume that these 9 leaders probably do behave differently as leaders, we may then ask how well (or how consistently) the various scales discriminate among these leadership styles. We do not know whether these leaders differ in leadership style, and this must remain a bare assumption. We should note, however, that the evaluation scores of the 9 leaders (scores which are significantly associated, in Table 4, with leadership style) were tested both for homogeneity of variance and for between-leader differences, using the evaluations provided by the teachers on the specific leader behavior forms. Bartlett's chi square test revealed that the assumption of homogeneity of variance was tenable; and the subsequent analysis of variance between groups yielded an F ratio of 2.374, which is significant at the .05 level.

We consider the general scales first, and present in Table 5 the

TABLE 5—Bartlett's Chi Square Test for Homogeneity of Variance, and Analysis of Variance Among Nine Communities, for Initiating Structure and Consideration Scales (N = 63)

Scale	Chi Square Value for Bartlett's Test	Analysis of Variance				
		Source of Variance	Sum of Squares	Degrees of Freedom	Estimated Variance	"F" Ratio
Initiating Structure	12.89	Between groups Within groups Total	48.15 176.76 224.91	8 54 62	6.019 3.273	1.839
Consideration	26.49[a]	Between groups Within groups Total	19.19 311.04 340:23	8 54 62	3.649 5.750	.634

[a] Significant at the .01 level of confidence.

data on homogeneity of variance and between-group discrimination for the two general measures, initiating structure and consideration. This table (and all subsequent tables, whether for the general or specific scales) is based upon a total of 63 describers in 9 communities, where 4 of the communities had 4 describers each, and the remaining 5 communities had 6, 7, 8, 12 and 14 describers respectively.

Table 5 indicates that neither of the two general measures discriminates significantly among the 9 leaders; and that for the initiating structure scores the assumption of homogeneity of variance is

TABLE 6—Bartlett's Chi Square Test for Homogeneity of Variance, and Analysis of Variance Among Nine Communities, for Four Specific Leader Behavior Description Scales (N = 63)

Scale	Chi Square Value for Bartlett's Test	Analysis of Variance				
		Source of Variance	Sum of Squares	Degrees of Freedom	Estimated Variance	"F" Ratio
Communication	6.253	Between groups Within groups Total	69.00 119.22 188.22	8 54 62	8.625 2.208	3.906[b]
Separatism	4.126	Between groups Within groups Total	41.49 163.94 205.43	8 54 62	5.186 3.029	1.712
Change	16.765[a]	Between groups Within groups Total	65.03 170.91 235.94	8 54 62	8.129 3.165	2.568[a]
Domination	6.652	Between groups Within groups Total	49.35 184.97 234.32	8 54 62	6.189 3.425	1.801

[a] Significant at the .05 level of confidence.
[b] Significant at the .01 level of confidence.

tenable, while for consideration this assumption is not tenable (since the chi square value is significant at the .01 level of confidence). These results regarding homogeneity of variance are parallel to those obtained by Halpin (4) in his study of 50 school executives who were described both by board members and by teachers. He examined the homogeneity of variance of both board and teacher descriptions of these executives, using the same two leadership measures, and concluded:

> "We find that on Consideration, for both staff and board taken separately, the variance with which the respondent groups describe their

respective superintendents differs significantly between groups. But with the Initiating Structure scores, the assumption of homogeneity of variance is tenable."

Halpin goes on to note that efforts to reduce this heterogeneity of variance for the consideration scores by the use of a square root transformation were not successful; nor, by inspection, did other orthodox transformations appear useful. For our limited sample, then, it appears that the two general scales do not discriminate among the 9 leaders; and the variances, in the case of the consideration scores, are widely disparate.

The parallel data on homogeneity of variance and between-group discrimination for the specific scales are presented in Table 6. On 3 of the 4 leadership measures, the assumption of homogeneity of variance is tenable; and the remaining chi square is significant at the .05 level. The variance analyses indicate that two of the dimensions discriminate significantly among the 9 leaders; but the results for the "change" scores (significant discrimination at the .05 level) must be cautiously interpreted in light of the fact that this is the one dimension on which the homogeneity assumption is most questionable.

SUMMARY

No one would presume to choose between two kinds of leader behavior scales on the basis of the minimal evidence provided here; and we wish to make it quite clear that this paper is not intended as such an evaluation of the general and specific scales. Not only is the sample too small for that, but the scales themselves have undergone different kinds and degrees of refinement, and the specific scales have been used only in the educational situation. That revealing work can be done with both types of scales seems to us to have been amply demonstrated both in this monograph and elsewhere (6, 9). It is, furthermore, entirely likely that the purposes of the investigator as well as the demands of the situation under investigation, will have much to do with decisions that are made about the proper research instruments.

With these caveats quite firmly in mind, however, our comparative data yield evidence upon which we may project some future concerns in the measurement of leadership style. The first and most obvious of these is the need for behavioral validation of both types of instruments we have been dealing with in this paper. Though there are a good many parallels in the results obtained through the two forms, there is enough difference to suggest that we need to know more precisely how well these instruments detect differences in leadership style which might be observed in more direct ways than staff report. For this sample, the general scales show no reliable differences among the 9 leaders; while the specific scales suggest that there may be such differences. The differences shown by the specific scales may constitute a more realistic picture, occasioned by the more sharply focussed nature of the question. On the other hand, these reported differences in leadership style may be a function of the fact that we have, by chance, selected a group of teachers whose evaluation of the given leaders is significantly different from the evaluation of those who used the general scale; and these differences in the evaluation of the leader then show up in the teachers' descriptions of leadership style.

A second point of concern which our analysis highlights is the question of relatively gross as against fine discriminations in leadership style. It is apparent from the evidence presented elsewhere in this volume that the general scales can, under given conditions, discriminate among leadership styles. But if we assume that the nine leaders in our sample are, indeed, different in some important respects in the way they lead, the general scales apparently cannot detect such differences. To say that they cannot means that either they require a larger sample of respondents per unit (to take care among other things of relatively large variances in description within units), or that the general scales represent rather gross measures of leadership differentia and thus do not catch the subtler variations which (we are presuming) do indeed characterize the leaders in question. Whether these subtler variations are important will depend, of course, upon the nature of the hypotheses to be tested.

Finally, though there may be some hope that the specific scales can make such discriminations while at the same time minimizing the halo problem (by pin-pointing the behavior being described) there is little evidence in this study that this is more than hope. The specific scales correlate as highly with the evaluation scores as, for example, does consideration; the intercorrelation among the 4 specific scales are generally (though not uniformly) somewhat higher than those for the general scales; and the significant differences in leadership style which the specific scales report are parallel by significant differences in evaluation scores. All this does not *demonstrate* halo (since a high degree of uniformity in various leadership dimensions may, indeed, be the rule; and, further, the correlations with evaluation may point not to halo, but to the fact that particular styles of leadership are commonly accepted or rejected); but it does lead one to be wary on this point.

Indeed, perhaps the sum of his paper, with all its limitations, is that we do need to be wary—wary of the results obtained by any leadership instrument where we have a minimal number of describers (and this, for many reasons, is the usual rather than the atypical case); wary of restricting ourselves to relatively gross distinctions in leadership style; and wary of the rather easy assumption that particular kinds of instruments (e.g. those which specify content) will readily solve the problem of halo in leadership description. We have apparently, a very long way yet to go in our efforts to develop leadership scales which are sensitive indicators of performance.

REFERENCES

1. Campbell, D. T. "The Indirect Assessment of Attitudes," *Psychological Bulletin*, 1950, *47*, 15–38.
2. Fleischman, E. A., Harris, E. F., and Burtt, H. E. *Leadership and Supervision in Industry*. Columbus, Ohio: Bureau of Educational Research, Ohio State University, 1955.
3. Halpin, A. W. "The Leader Behavior and Leadership Ideology of Educational Administrators and Aircraft Commanders." *Harvard Educational Review*, 1955, *25*, 18–32.
4. Halpin, A. W. *The Leadership Behavior of School Superintendents*. Columbus. The Ohio State University, Department of Education. 1956 (mimeographed).
5. Hammond, K. R. "Measuring Attitudes by Error-Choice." *Journal of Abnormal and Social Psychology*, 1948, *43*, 38–48.
6. Hemphill, J. K. "Leadership Behavior Associated with the Administrative Reputation of College Departments." *Journal of Educational Psychology*, 1955, *46*, 385–401.
7. Myrdal, G. *An American Dilemma*. New York: Harper and Brothers, 1944.
8. Seeman, M. *A Status Factor Approach to Leadership*. Columbus, Ohio: Personnel Research Board, The Ohio State University, 1950 (mimeographed).

9. Seeman, M. "Role Conflict and Ambivalence in Leadership." *American Sociological Review,* 1953, *18,* 373–380.
10. Seeman, M. *Leadership in American Society: The Case of the School Executive,* (forthcoming).
11. Wherry, R. J. "Control of Bias in Rating: III, Factor Analysis of Rating Item Indices." Final Report, RF Project 417, The Ohio State University, 1951 (mimeographed).

IX

A LEADER BEHAVIOR DESCRIPTION FOR INDUSTRY

Edwin A. Fleishman

Yale University

Previous sections have described the developmental history of the Leader Behavior Description Questionnaire and its subsequent use in certain military and other situations. The problems of leadership and supervision in industry are to a great extent parallel to those found in military and educational institutions, and no less important. Similarly, the need is just as great for adequate procedures to describe in functional terms how the foreman, supervisor, or executive deals with people in his leadership role.

This study is concerned with the development and application of a Leader Behavior Description for use primarily in industry. The original work on this form of the questionnaire was carried out in connection with a larger project on leadership in industry sponsored by the International Harvester Company at the Personnel Research Board (4,5,6,9). Specifically, it is the purpose of this paper to summarize the evidence now available on the industrial form of the questionnaire, and to evaluate its reliability and validity.

DEVELOPMENT OF THE SUPERVISORY BEHAVIOR DESCRIPTION

As indicated in previous sections, the Leader Behavior Description started with over 1,800 items and was reduced to 150 items by "expert judges" who sorted them into 9 "a priori" dimensions of leadership behavior (e.g., integration, representation, fraternization). Subsequent administration of the original form yielded high correlations among these dimensions indicating the need for a reorganization of the items into fewer and more independent categories of leader behavior. The subsequent factor analysis of the items, carried out for this purpose has been described in Section II. It will be recalled that this analysis was based on descriptions by 300 Air Force crew members who described their aircraft commanders. Historically, the development of the industrial form of the questionnaire begins immediately after the completion of this analysis based on the Air Force data and parallels the development of the final Air Force form. Up to this point the Air Force and industrial forms have the same developmental history. From this point on, the construction of the industrial and Air Force forms followed their own lines of development. In fact, work on the final industrial and Air Force forms of the questions was carried out independently at about the same time.

CONSTRUCTION OF THE PRELIMINARY INDUSTRIAL FORM

It will be recalled that the factor analysis of the Leader Behavior Description items, based on Air Force data, yielded two major factors together with two minor factors. The major factors were defined as "Consideration" and "Initiating Structure" and these accounted for more than 80 per cent of the common variance among the 150 items. Items loaded on the "Consideration" factor described behavior indicative of friendship, mutual trust and respect, and good "human relations" between the leader and his group. Items loaded on the "Initiating Structure" factor denoted behavior of the leader in organizing and defining the relationships between himself and the group, in defining interactions among group members, establishing ways of getting the job done, scheduling, criticizing, etc. The minor factors were tentatively labeled "Production Emphasis" and "Social Sensitivity."

For the industrial form of this questionnaire, new keys were developed from inspection of the rotated matrix of factor loadings provided by the Air Force analysis. Items with the highest loadings and purest factor structure were selected for each key corresponding to each of the four factors. These new keys, based on the Air Force population data, were used as the starting point for the construction and later revision of a Supervisory Behavior Description for use in industry. Henceforth, the industrial form of the Leader Behavior Description questionnaire will be referred to as the Supervisory Behavior Description.

PRETESTING THE PRELIMINARY QUESTIONNAIRE

A 136-item *Supervisory Behavior Description* questionnaire was administered to a pre-test sample of 100 International Harvester foremen at the Company's Central School in Chicago. These foremen, representing 17 different plants, used the questionnaire to describe the behavior of their own supervisors. Their average age was 41.5 years. The average length of time in the company was 14.3 years, and the average length of time as a foreman was 5.9 years. The average number of men they supervised was 29.7 men.

The questionnaires were scored along the new factor dimensions derived from the Air Force sample. The purpose of the industrial pilot study was to determine the usefulness of these new scales in an industrial population, and to determine what further revision would be necessary to make them applicable. Table 1 presents the reliabilities and intercorrelations of the four dimension scores, as well as the means and standard deviations.

TABLE 1—Intercorrelations and Reliabilities of the Pre-Test Supervisory Behavior Description Dimension Scores (N = 100)

Dimension	Dimension			
	1	2	3	4
	r	r	r	r
1. Consideration		.56	.64	.66
2. Initiating Structure	.56		.80	.67
3. Production Emphasis	.64	.80		.69
4. Social Sensitivity	.66	.67	.69	
Reliability	.95	.89	.76	.77
Mean	30.33	18.68	9.74	1.84
Standard Deviation	22.99	11.94	8.52	7.76
Number of Items	40	24	22	20

Intercorrelations of the dimension scores showed that they still had substantial overlap with one another when applied to this industrial sample. This may have resulted for several reasons. The foremen may have responded to certain items in each key according to their own judgment of "What is a good leader," instead of simply describing their own supervisor's behavior. This is the "halo effect" so common to instruments of this type. The more "halo," the higher the correlation between dimension scores. A second reason may be that in this sample, certain of the items in the various scales may have high loadings on several factors. Or, on the other hand, an item previously assigned to one dimension may in this industrial sample correlate more highly with a dimension in which it was not scored.

Another reason for the high dimension intercorrelations may be that the factor structure on which the keys were based is not the same for this population. In other words, the categories of leader behavior which are most independent in this industrial population may be very different from those which were most independent in the Air Force population data.

ITEM ANALYSIS

In order to clarify some of these problems, a statistical analysis was carried out at the item level. Two kinds of information were obtained concerning each of the 36 items in the Supervisory Behavior Description Questionnaire.

First, the distributions of responses among the five choices for each item were considered. Second, tetrachoric correlations of every item with each dimension total score were calculated to give indices of the internal consistency of the dimensions, and to reveal the sources of overlap between the dimensions. Thus, coefficients were not only computed between an item and its own dimension total score, but also between it and the total scores of the other three dimensions to which it had *not* been assigned. Of the 136 items in the Supervisory Behavior Description, only 106 were included in the four keys. The remaining 30 items were not scored in any dimension. This analysis revealed that most of the items correlated highly with the total score of the dimension to which they were assigned. However, it was also evident that most of the items correlated highly with one or more dimensions to which they were not assigned.

The item-dimension correlations were considered as the assumed factor loadings of the items on the four oblique (correlated) factors following the rationale provided in the Wherry-Gaylord factor analysis procedure (13). In order to compare the loadings and factor structure with that obtained from the Air Force population, some rotation of factors seemed to be necessary. Transformation to orthogonality was accomplished and it appeared, by inspection, that this transformation brought the loadings more in line with the original factors derived from the Air Force factor analysis. Loadings of items increased on dimensions to which the items were assigned and decreased on other dimensions. This seemed especially true for the two major factors (Consideration and Initiating Structure). Further preliminary rotations were then made with the primary objective of rotating the items originally in the two minor factors into more independent clusters. It appeared that this might not be possible, and in the light of the high correlations between these factors and the other two, their utility was questioned for this population. Practically all the variation could be accounted for by the two major dimensions.

CONSTRUCTION OF THE REVISED QUESTIONNAIRE

Based on the item-dimension loadings derived from this industrial sample, two revised scoring keys were developed—one for "Consideration" and one for "Initiating Structure." Criteria for item inclusion were (1) the item should have a high loading with the dimension in which it was to be included, (2) the item should have as close to zero loading as possible on the other factor, (3) items which did not discriminate among supervisors should be rejected.

Twenty-eight items best meeting these criteria for "Consideration" and 20 items for "Initiating Structure" were selected. Table 2 presents the items finally selected for the revised form. The loadings given are those derived from the industrial sample.

It can be seen that most of the items assigned to each key have high loadings with that dimension and insignificant loadings with the other. In addition, one more step was carried out. It was possible to select items for the "Initiating Structure" key so that some items had small *negative* loadings on "Consideration," and others had small *positive* loadings on "Consideration." It was hoped that the total effect of this would be to cancel out or "suppress" further the unwanted variance in the "Initiating Structure" key due to these cumulative small loadings on "Consideration." Another thing that was done was to change slightly a word or two in certain items which seemed to affect the unwanted variance slightly. For example, an item "He suggests new approaches to problems" was loaded highly on "Initiating Structure" but it had some loading on "Con-

TABLE 2—Items Selected for the Revised Form of the Supervisory Behavior Description

Item Number	Item	Orthogonal Factor Loading[a]	
		Consideration	Initiating Structure
	CONSIDERATION: REVISED KEY		
2.	*He refuses to give in when people disagree with him.	—.68	.06
4.	*He does personal favors for the foremen under him.	.40	.06
6.	*He expresses appreciation when one of us does a good job.	.70	.19
18.	*He is easy to understand.	.70	.13
22.	*He demands more than we can do.	—.40	—.08
26.	*He helps his foremen with their personal problems.	.32	.05
27.	*He criticizes his foremen in front of others.	—.49	.03
28.	He stands up for his foremen even though it makes him unpopular.	.54	.08
32.	*He insists that everything be done his way.	—.52	—.01
36.	He sees that a foreman is rewarded for a job well done.	.70	—.05
47.	*He rejects suggestions for changes.	—.62	—.06
57.	He changes the duties of people under him without first talking it over with them.	—.69	.09
64.	*He treats people under him without considering their feelings.	—.72	.41
70.	*He tries to keep the foremen under him in good standing with those in higher authority.	.68	.17
72.	He resists changes in ways of doing things.	—.57	—.16
76.	He "rides" the foreman who makes a mistake.	—.61	.37
87.	*He refuses to explain his actions.	—.72	.23
95.	He acts without consulting his foreman first.	—.73	.01
98.	*He stresses the importance of high morale among those under him.	.73	—.11
100.	*He backs up his foremen in their actions.	.62	.16
101.	*He is slow to accept new ideas.	—.66	—.06
105.	*He treats all his foremen as his equal.	.66	.28
107.	He criticizes a specific act rather than a particular individual.	.63	.14
108.	*He is willing to make changes.	.78	.09
111.	*He makes those under him feel at ease when talking with him.	.86	.17
112.	*He is friendly and can be easily approached.	.82	—.02
114.	*He puts suggestions that are made by foremen under him into operation.	.87	.11
124.	*He gets the approval of his foremen on important matters before going ahead.	.65	—.02
	INITIATING STRUCTURE: REVISED KEY		
8.	*He encourages overtime work.	.20	.40
9.	*He tries out his new ideas.	—.10	.42
11.	*He rules with an iron hand.	—.20	.58
14.	*He criticizes poor work.	—.18	.59
15.	*He talks about how much should be done.	—.20	.60
29.	He encourages slow-working foremen to greater effort.	.17	.33
30.	He waits for his foremen to push new ideas before he does.	—.07	—.28

TABLE 2—Continued

Item Number	Item	Orthogonal Factor Loading[a]	
		Consideration	Initiating Structure
31.	*He assigns people under him to particular tasks.	.00	.26
37.	He asks for sacrifices from his foremen for the good of the entire department.	.00	.46
39.	He insists that his foremen follow standard ways of doing things in every detail.	.25	.72
46.	*He sees to it that people under him are working up to their limits.	—.17	.87
63.	He offers new approaches to problems.	.36	.72
73.	*He insists that he be informed on decisions made by foremen under him.	.13	.51
81.	He lets others do their work the way they think best.	—.17	—.33
84.	He stresses being ahead of competing work groups.	.03	.34
93.	*He "needles" foremen under him for greater effort.	—.17	.50
103.	He decides in detail what shall be done and how it shall be done.	.37	.63
117.	He emphasizes meeting of deadlines.	.10	.68
128.	He asks foremen who have slow groups to get more out of their groups.	—.22	.40
133.	He emphasizes the quantity of work.	.17	.51

* Indicates item originally in that key (based on factor analysis of Air Force population data).
[a] Orthogonal loading based on this industrial pre-tested population.

sideration" also. By changing the word *suggests* to "He *offers* new approaches to problems," it was hoped that the slight loading on "Consideration" would be further reduced, yielding a "purer" item for the "Structure" scale.

ADMINISTRATION OF THE REVISED QUESTIONNAIRE

This 48-item revised Supervisory Behavior Description was next administered to another comparable sample of 122 foremen in one of the Harvester Company's Motor Truck Manufacturing plants. Again, the subjects were to use the questionnaire to describe the behavior of their own immediate supervisor in the plant. The purpose of this administration was to check on the characteristics of the questionnaire in its revised form in terms of range of scores achieved, reliabilities, and the degree of independence achieved for the two keys.

In this final form of the questionnaire, alternatives for each item were weighted from zero to four, in place of the -2 to $+2$ weights used for each item in the preliminary form. Thus, the highest possible score was 112 for Consideration (28 items), and 80 for Initiating Structure (20 items). As before, assurances were given the foremen that no one in the company would see their answers.

TABLE 3—Means, Standard Deviations, Range, Reliabilities, and Intercorrelations of the Dimension Scores in the Revised Supervisory Behavior Description

Statistical Measure	Dimension	
	Consideration	Initiating Structure
Number of Items	28	20
Mean	82.26	51.50
Standard Deviation	15.47	8.75
Range	22 to 106	13 to 68
Reliability	.92	.68
Intercorrelation	—.02	

Table 3 presents the results obtained for 122 foremen. From the results on this sample, it was obvious that the two dimensions were now quite independent of each other ($r = -.02$), that adequate internal consistency reliability was achieved for each dimension key, and that the questionnaire yielded a wide range of scores on each dimension. The usual "halo effect" from scale to scale that occurs in most instruments in this area, seemed for the most part to have been eliminated.

An additional check on the adequacy of the revised questionnaire was carried out with this same sample. This concerned the agreement achieved among different respondents who described the same supervisor's behavior. The variation in scores obtained was divided into (1) variance between descriptions of different foremen, and (2) variance within descriptions of the same foreman. This "within description" variation represents lack of agreement among respondents describing the same supervisor. The analysis of variance comparing these two variance estimates revealed significantly less variation among respondents describing the same supervisor than between descriptions of different supervisors. This appeared to be further evidence of the objectivity of the questionnaire procedure.

Evidence that each scale of the Supervisory Behavior Description measures a single factor has been presented. Table 4 summarizes the data available on the internal consistency of these scales as meas-

TABLE 4—Summary of Internal Consistency Reliabilities[a] Obtained with the Supervisory Behavior Description from Various Samples

N	Sample	Supervisor Described	Dimension	
			Consideration	Initiating Structure
			r	r
394	Employees	First Line Foremen	.98	.78
122	Foremen	General Foremen	.92	.68
176	ROTC Cadets	Other Cadets and Superior Officers	.89	.81

[a] Split-half correlations (between totals for odd and even numbered items within each scale, corrected for full length of each scale).

ured by the split-half technique. These reliabilities represent the correlations of odd numbered items with even numbered items corrected for full length of the scale by the Spearman-Brown formula.

It is to be noted that the reliability of the two scales is maintained when applied to ROTC cadets as well as industrial samples, and also holds up at different levels in the industrial hierarchy. It is also seen that the Consideration scale is somewhat more reliable, and this is only partly a function of the fact that this scale is slightly longer than the Initiating Structure scale.

INTER-RATER AGREEMENT

The split-half reliability estimates gave evidence of the consistency of individual descriptions. Table 5 summarizes the evidence on

TABLE 5—Summary of Inter-Rater Agreement Coefficients Obtained With the Supervisory Behavior Description from Various Samples

Sample	Type of Coefficient	Dimension	
		Consideration	Initiating Structure
		r	r
Workers Describing 59 Foremen	Horst	.55	.50
Workers Describing 31 Foremen	Epsilon	.72	.64
Foremen Describing 60 General Foremen	Epsilon	.65	.47
ROTC Cadets Describing 176 Cadets and Superior Officers	Horst	.64	.64

reliability regarded as agreement among descriptions by different people of the same supervisors. This type of reliability is crucial since often we must depend on a small number of descriptions of each supervisor. As can be seen, two types of coefficients are represented. The unbiased correlation ratio (ε) is derived from an analysis of variance of between-description variation, relative to within-description variance. The procedure and rationale for converting the F ratio obtained to ε, which indicates the strength of relationship, is presented by Peters and Van Voorhis (12). The Horst Coefficient of inter-rater agreement (11) is more generally known and yields results in the same general range. The number of people rating the same supervisor varied from 3 to 14 per supervisor in these samples. It is obvious that significant agreement among respondents using the Supervisory Behavior Description was achieved for both the "Consideration" and "Structure" scales in all samples.

TEST-RETEST RELIABILITY

On the basis of repeated measurements, some limited evidence is available on the questionnaire's reliability viewed in terms of stability over time. Table 6 summarizes some of these data. Descrip-

TABLE 6—Summary of Test-Retest Reliability Coefficients Obtained With the Supervisory Behavior Description from Various Samples

Sample	Time Between Administrations	Dimension	
		Consideration	Initiating Structure
		r	r
Workers Describing 18 Foremen[a]	11 months	.87	.75
Workers Describing 59 Foremen[b]	11 months	.58	.46
Workers Describing 31 Foremen[b]	3 weeks	.56	.53

[a] Descriptions of foremen by the same workers during test and retest.
[b] Descriptions of foremen by different workers during test and retest.

tions were obtained for one group of 59 foremen at the beginning and end of an 11-month period. For another group of 31 foremen an interval of 3 weeks intervened between the two administrations. It should be pointed out that at least three descriptions were obtained from workers under each of these foremen during each administration. However, different workers were drawn randomly from each foreman's work group during each administration of the questionnaire. This, of course, would tend to lower the correlations between descriptions of these foremen from one administration to the next. Nevertheless, as can be seen in Table 6, the retest coefficients even after an 11-month period are substantial when one considers that their magnitude is about as high as the inter-rater agreement.

It was possible to locate 18 workers who were included in the first and second administrations of the questionnaire where 11 months intervened. It can be seen that descriptions of foremen made by these workers had a test-retest reliability of .87 and .75 for "Consideration" and "Initiating Structure" respectively. These are of the same general magnitude as the internal consistency reliabilities of these scales presented in Table 4.

These test-retest findings have additional implications beyond those of statistical reliability. They present evidence that leadership patterns in the industrial situation, as measured by this questionnaire, are highly stable over time, and that measurements on these scales taken at one point in time may be generalized, within limits, to subsequent leader behavior in the same situation. An additional point to stress is that when training intervenes between measurements of supervisory behavior, there is a marked shrinkage in the test-retest coefficients. For the present samples, no training intervened. These findings and their implications have been discussed in some detail by Fleishman and associates (7, 9).

INTERCORRELATIONS BETWEEN THE LEADERSHIP SCALES

As indicated earlier, the questionnaire was constructed to yield independent measures of two important leadership dimensions, "Consideration" and "Initiating Structure." The final revised form was constructed on the basis of data obtained from one foreman sample and then administered to another sample of 122 foremen who described their own supervisors in the plant. The correlation between "Consideration" and "Structure" was found to be −.02, confirming the independence of the scales in a sample comparable to the standardization sample. In addition, the questionnaire was administered to 394 workers who described these 122 foremen. In this case, the correlation between scales was −.33. Although somewhat higher than the r obtained from descriptions filled out by foremen, this coefficient is still lower than that obtained in previous revisions.

Data were also available from a sample of 176 Air Force and Army ROTC students who described their superior officers. The correlation between the two scales in this sample was −.05. These additional data confirm that these two dimensions are most usefully considered orthogonal coordinates against which the behavior of leaders in different situations may be plotted.

VALIDITY OF THE SUPERVISORY BEHAVIOR DESCRIPTION

Another way of assessing the utility of the Supervisory Behavior Description is in terms of correlations with independent measures of leadership effectiveness. Correlations with industrial criteria were obtained in one of the International Harvester Company's plants. The detailed development and purification of these criteria has been described by Fleishman, Harris and Burtt (7). Correlations were obtained between descriptions of foreman behavior and independent indices of accident rates, absenteeism, grievances, and turnover among the foreman's own work groups. Correlations were also obtained between foreman behavior descriptions and ratings of foreman proficiency by management. In addition, to these industrial criteria, Bass and Coates (2) have provided correlations for ROTC cadets between the Supervisory Behavior Description and (a) subsequent performance on situational leadership tests as represented by the leaderless group discussion technique, and (b) subsequent leadership ratings by fellow cadets and superior officers. Table 7 summarizes the results for foremen, and Table 8 shows the data for ROTC students.

TABLE 7—Correlations Between the Supervisory Behavior Dimensions and Various Industrial Criteria of Leadership Effectiveness

Criterion	Department	Dimension	
		Consideration	Initiating Structure
		r	r
Proficiency Ratings by	Production Foremen	—.31[b]	.47[b]
Foremen's Supervisor	Nonproduction Foremen	.28	—.19
Absenteeism by Foremen's	Production Foremen	—.49[b]	.27[a]
Work Group	Nonproduction Foremen	—.38	.06
Accidents by Foremen's	Production Foremen	—.06	.15
Work Group	Nonproduction Foremen	—.42[a]	.18
Formal Grievances by Foremen's	Production Foremen	—.07	.45[b]
Work Group	Nonproduction Foremen	.15	.23
Turnover in Foremen's	Production Foremen	.13	.06
Work Group	Nonproduction Foremen	.04	.51[a]

$N = 72$ production departments and 23 nonproduction departments.
[a] Significant at .05 level of confidence.
[b] Significant at .01 level of confidence.

TABLE 8—Correlations of Supervisory Behavior Dimensions With Other Measures for ROTC Cadets

Measure	N	Dimension	
		Consideration	Initiating Structure
Ratings by Peers[a]	176	.33[c]	.18[d]
Ratings by Superiors[a]	133	.00	—.06
Situational-Test (LDG)[b]	133	—.25[c]	.32[c]
Situational Test Later[b]	165	—.15[d]	.12
Scholastic Achievement (3 Year College Grade Point Average)	133	—.09	—.06
ACE Quantitative plus Language Scores	133	—.04	.14
Gestalt Completion	75	—.02	.05
Concealed Figures	107	.15	.19[d]
F Scale	165	—.03	—.29[c]

[a] These ratings were made in terms of "value to the group."
[b] Score obtained was "amount of successful leadership activity displayed."
[c] Significant at the .01 level of confidence.
[d] Significant at the .05 level of confidence.

Table 7 indicates the differential relationships between Consideration and/or Initiating Structure and the various industrial criteria. It can also be seen that marked differences were obtained in production departments compared with nonproduction departments. In production departments, high scores on the Consideration scale were predictive of low ratings of proficiency by the foreman's supervisor, but low absenteeism among the workers. A high score on "Initiating Structure" was predictive of a high proficiency rating, but high absenteeism and labor grievances as well. Among nonproduction foremen, a high score on "Consideration" was predictive of low accident rates with a trend toward low absenteeism as well. A high score on "Initiating Structure" was related to high labor turnover in nonproduction departments.

Among ROTC cadets, the Supervisory Behavior Description was predictive of ratings by peers, where a high score in both Consideration and Structure was related to high leadership ratings. In the leaderless group discussion situation, the Structure scale was also related to high leadership scores, but the Consideration score was negatively related to success in this situation.

Although the need for additional evidence is great, there is sufficient evidence here that the Supervisory Behavior Description scores are predictive of other independent leadership criteria. It may also be pointed out that the measures on the scales may themselves be used as criteria where it is desired to predict certain kinds of leadership behavior from other predictor variables (e.g., personality measures).

CORRELATIONS WITH OTHER MEASURES

Only scanty data exist regarding the relationships between Supervisory Behavior Description scores and aptitude and personality measures. Table 8 summarizes data obtained with ROTC cadets, in which correlations were obtained between descriptions of cadets and scores on other measures made by the cadets described.

It is obvious from these results that the leadership descriptions did not depend at all on the "intelligence" of the cadet described as

TABLE 9—Means and Standard Deviations of Supervisory Behavior Description Scores

Sample	Dimension			
	Consideration		Initiating Structure	
	M	S.D.	M	S.D.
Descriptions of 122 Foremen	79.8	14.5	41.5	7.6
Descriptions of 31 Foremen	71.5	13.2	37.5	6.3
Descriptions of 31 Foremen	73.0	12.7	40.7	7.3
Descriptions of 8 Civil Service Supervisors	75.1	17.6	37.3	9.6
Descriptions of 60 General Foremen	82.3	15.5	51.5	8.8

measured by the cadet's three-year college grade-point average or by his total ACE score. The remaining 3 tests were included by Bass and Coates (2) as measures of perceptual flexibility which was hypothesized as related to leadership patterns. The Gestalt Completion requires the subject to identify a series of mutilated figures. The subject must organize the pattern into a meaningful whole where he does not know what figures he is looking for. This test represents the speed of closure factor (8), which has been described as the ability to unify an apparently disparate perceptual field into a simple percept. As can be seen in Table 9, no significant relationship was found between this test and either leadership dimension.

The Concealed Figures Test requires the subject to indicate whether or not a certain stimulus is imbedded in a series of more complex figures. This factor has been termed "Speed of Closure" and seems to involve keeping in mind a definite configuration in spite of the fact that the perceptual field contains a lot of distracting perceptual material. This test had only a low, but significant, correlation with the Initiating Structure scale. Apparently, there may be some tendency for people with this ability to do more organizing, planning, evaluating, etc., in their leadership role. This hypothesis is worthy of further exploration.

The F scale measure of authoritarianism (1) was included as a third measure of flexibility and ability to cope with ambiguity. Surprisingly, this scale correlated negatively with the "Structure" key of the Supervisory Behavior Description. However, these findings are consistent with those of Hollander (10) who found negative relations between authoritarian tendencies and leadership ratings by peers among Naval cadets. Bass and Coates (2) suggest that persons high on the F scale may be less able to make decisions in ambiguous situations and may be more likely to accept the structure which develops. A need for experimental attack on these possibilities is indicated.

Other correlations between these scales and certain other variables were obtained for foremen at Harvester. These results indicated no significant correlation between the two scales and the foreman's education, age, time with the company, time as a supervisor, or number of men supervised. On the other hand, previous results (6,7) in industry have shown that scores achieved by foremen on the Supervisory Behavior Description are highly related to scores achieved by their own supervisors in the plant on the same leadership dimensions.

NORMATIVE DATA

It is hoped that future use of the questionnaire will provide normative data as a basis for future comparisons of leader behavior patterns in specified situations. Such data do not exist at present. Table 9 summarizes what data are available currently on means and standard deviations found in a number of samples with the questionnaire.

It can be seen that the three foremen samples all score lower in "Consideration" as well as "Initiating Structure" than does the sample of supervisors a step above the foremen level. Moreover, the small sample of first-line civil service employees achieved scores comparable to those achieved by first-line industrial foremen. These data are no substitute for more extensive normative data, but they furnish at least some basis for comparison.

SUMMARY

This section has pulled together all the available evidence on the Supervisory Behavior Description, which was developed for use in industry. Its evolvement from earlier research on the Leader Behavior Description was described and its properties evaluated. Like the Air Force version, the final industrial form measures "Consideration" and "Initiating Structure." These scales were shown to be independent and reliable. Reliability was assessed in terms of internal consistency, inter-rater agreement, and stability of repeated measurements over time. Validity was assessed through correlations with independent leadership measures, such as objective group indices (absenteeism, turnover), productivity ratings, peer ratings, and leaderless group situation tests. The scales were found differentially predictive of a number of these criteria. Correlations with other measures revealed that the scores achieved were independent of certain measures of general intelligence. The low correlations between the scales and other psychometric and background measures, and the substantial correlation with certain leadership criteria, suggest that these scales may be useful additions in the fields of leadership research and assessment.

REFERENCES

1. Adorno, T. W., Frenkel-Brunswick, E., et al. *The Authoritarian Personality*. New York: Harpers, 1950.
2. Bass, B. M., and Coates, C. H. *Situational and Personality Factors in Leadership in ROTC*. Baton Rouge: Louisiana State University. Unpublished manuscript.
3. Fleishman, E. A. *Leadership Climate and Supervisory Behavior*. Columbus, Ohio: Personnel Research Board, Ohio State University, 1951. Out of print report.
4. Fleishman, E. A. The Description of Supervisory Behavior. *J. appl. Psychol.*, 1953, *36*, 1–6.
5. Fleishman, E. A. The Measurement of Leadership Attitudes in Industry. *J. Appl. Psychol.*, 1953, *36*, 153–158.
6. Fleishman, E. A. Leadership Climate, Human Relations Training, and Supervisory Behavior. *Personnel Psychol.*, 1953, *6*, 205–222.

7. Fleishman, E. A., Harris, E. F., and Burtt, H. E. *Leadership and Supervision in Industry*. Columbus, Ohio: Bureau of Educational Research, Ohio State University, 1955.
8. French, J. W. (Ed.). *Manual for Kit of Selected Tests for Reference Aptitude and Achievement Factors*. Educational Testing Service, Princeton, N. J. 1954.
9. Harris, E. F., and Fleishman, E. A. Human Relations Training and the Stability of Leadership Patterns. *J. Appl. Psychol.*, 1955, *39*, 20–25.
10. Hollander, E. P. Authoritarianism and Leadership Choice in a Military Setting. *Amer. Psychol.*, 1953, *8*, 368 (abstract).
11. Horst, P. A Generalized Expression for the Reliability of Measures. *Psychometrika*, 1949, *14*, 21–23.
12. Peters, C. C., and Van Voorhis, M. A. *Statistical Procedures and Their Mathematical Bases*. New York: McGraw-Hill, 1940.
13. Wherry, R. J., and Gaylord, R. H. The Concept of Test and Item Reliability in Relation to Factor Pattern. *Psychometrika*, 1953, *18*, 247–264.

X

THE LEADERSHIP OPINION QUESTIONNAIRE

Edwin A. Fleishman

Yale University

No less important than the description of leadership behavior is the assessment of leadership attitudes. Previous sections have described the procedures developed for the quantitative description of the leader's behavior as perceived by himself and others.

This section will describe the development and evaluation of a questionnaire for the measurement of leadership attitudes. The questionnaire, called the Leadership Opinion Questionnaire, is parallel to the Supervisory Behavior Description described in Section IX and measures the same two dimensions of Consideration and Initiating Structure. Like the Supervisory Behavior Description, this questionnaire was developed in connection with research at the Personnel Research Board in cooperation with the International Harvester Company (5,6,7,11). While not considered a substitute for the Supervisory Behavior Description, the Leadership Opinion Questionnaire is more easily administered and has actually been used in a greater variety of situations than has the Supervisory Behavior Description.

CONSTRUCTION AND PRETEST OF THE PRELIMINARY FORM

A preliminary 110 item Leadership Opinion Questionnaire was administered to a sample of 100 foremen, representing 17 different International Harvester Company plants. The foreman indicated for each item how frequently he thought he should do what each item described. He responded by marking one of 5 frequency alternatives which followed each item (e.g., always, often, occasionally, seldom, never). He was told that his responses should not necessarily indicate what he found himself actually doing, but more what he thought he should do in his relations with his work group. It was also emphasized that there were no right or wrong answers in the questionnaire since "everyone's work group is different and what is the best way to lead one group may not be the best way for another."

The items in this questionnaire were generally parallel to those in the pretest form of the Supervisory Behavior Description previously described, except these items were worded in terms of "what *should* you, as a supervisor, do?," rather than in terms of "what does your own supervisor actually do?." As in the case of the pretest Supervisory Behavior Description, the questionnaire was scored along the factors of Consideration, Initiating Structure, Production Emphasis, and Social Sensitivity, with items assigned to each key on the basis of the factor analysis of Air Force Leader Behavior Description items. As before, the 5 alternatives to each item were weighted zero to four. Total dimension scores were derived by adding the weights corresponding to the alternatives marked for the items in each dimension.

The corrected split-half reliability estimates for the two major keys "Consideration" and "Initiating Structure" were .69 and .73, respectively, and for the two minor keys "Production Emphasis" and "Social Sensitivity," .36 and .33, respectively. In the light of the low reliabilities of the latter two keys, and in view of the fact that a modified factor analysis of the items in the parallel Supervisory Behavior Description indicated that only two major dimensions were meaningful in this industrial population, the dimensions of "Production Emphasis" and "Social Sensitivity" were rejected from the revised form.

CONSTRUCTION OF THE REVISED QUESTIONNAIRE

The criteria for selecting items for the revised form included (a) the response distributions of the items in the Leadership Opinion Questionnaire obtained in the pretest, and (b) the factor loadings, based on this industrial sample, of parallel items on the Supervisory Behavior Description. Twenty items were selected in this manner for the "Consideration" key, and 20 items for the "Initiating Structure" key.

Table 1 shows the 20 items selected for each key of the revised Leadership Opinion Questionnaire. It should be noted that 18 of the 20 items in the "Consideration" key and 16 of the 20 items in the

TABLE 1—Items Selected for the Revised Form of the Leadership Opinion Questionnaire Key

CONSIDERATION: REVISED KEY

Refuse to compromise a point.
*Do personal favors for people in the work group.
Speak in a manner not to be questioned.
*Ask for more than members of the work group can get done.
*Help people in the work group with their personal problems.
Stand up for those in the work group under you, even though it makes you unpopular with others.
Insist that everything be done your way.
Reject suggestions for change.
*Change the duties of people in the work group without first talking it over with them.
**Resist changes in ways of doing things.
*Refuse to explain your actions.
*Act without consulting the work group.
Back up what people under you do.
Be slow to accept new ideas.
Treat all people in the work group as your equal.
Criticize a specific act rather that a particular member of the work group.
Be willing to make changes.
Put suggestions made by people in the work group into operation.
Get the approval of the work group on important matters before going ahead.
*Give in to others in discussions with your work group.

INITIATING STRUCTURE: REVISED KEY

*Encourage overtime work.
*Try out your own new ideas in the work group.
Rule with an iron hand.
Criticize poor work.
**Talk about how much should be done.
*Encourage slow-working people in the work group to work harder.
Wait for people in the work group to push new ideas.
Assign people in the work group to particular tasks.
*Ask for sacrifices from the men under you for the good of your entire section.
Ask that people under you follow to the letter those standard routines handed down to you.
*Offer new approaches to problems.
Put the section's welfare above the welfare of any member in it.
Insist that you be informed on decisions made by people in the work group under you.
Let others do their work the way they think best.
**Stress being ahead of competing work groups.
**"Needle" people in the work group for greater effort.
**Emphasize meeting of deadlines.
Decide in detail what shall be done and how it shall be done by the work group.
Meet with the group at regularly scheduled times.
See to it that people in the work group are working up to capacity.

Items not starred used the format:
    1. Always 2. Often 3. Occasionally 4. Seldom 5. Never.
Items starred (*) used the format:
    1. Often 2. Fairly often 3. Occasionally 4. Once in a while 5. Very seldom.
Items starred (**) used the format:
    1. A great deal 2. Fairly much 3. To some degree 4. Comparatively little 5. Not at all.

"Structure" key have parallel items on the Supervisory Behavior Description. It was not possible to select all the items from parallel items since the response distribution of certain items tended to be more skewed when the foremen used it to describe their own *attitudes* than in cases where they used it to describe the behavior of someone else. The following items and their comparative response distributions (number of people choosing each alternative) illustrate this point.

	Response Distribution				
Item	A Great Deal	Fairly Much	To Some Degree	Comparatively Little	Not at All
He stresses the importance of high morale among those under him. (Behavior scale)	39	28	28	5	0
Stress the importance of high morale in the work group. (Attitude scale)	72	17	10	1	0

Obviously the item did not do as good a job of discriminating in the attitude scale as it did in the behavior scale. In the few cases of this kind, items with greater discriminating power but similar in verbal content and factorial structure were selected for the revised Leadership Opinion Questionnaire.

ADMINISTRATION OF THE REVISED QUESTIONNAIRE

The revised 40-item questionnaire was administered to 122 foremen in one of the Harvester Company's plants. The foremen responded in terms of their own attitudes about how work groups should be led. Table 2 summarizes the means, standard deviations, ranges, and reliabilities for each dimension score, as well as the correlation between the two dimensions.

It can be seen that a wide range of scores was achieved on each dimension and that the reliabilities, although not exceptionally high, are adequate. The important thing in interpreting these reliability coefficients is their magnitude *relative* to the dimension intercorrelation. Apparently these instruments tap reliably two *independent* dimensions of leadership attitudes ($r = -.01$). This is especially interesting since a criterion for item inclusion was the loading of a

TABLE 2—Means, Standard Deviations, Range, Reliabilities, and Intercorrelation of the Dimension Scores in the Revised Leadership Opinion Questionnaire

Measure	Dimension	
	Consideration	Initiating Structure
Number of Items	20	20
Mean	53.9	53.3
Standard Deviation	7.2	7.8
Range[a]	36 to 74	34 to 69
Reliability[b]	.70	.79
Intercorrelation	—.01	

[a] Alternative responses for each item were weighted from zero to four. Thus, the highest possible score was 80 for each Dimension.
[b] Split-half correlations corrected to full length of each dimension by the Spearman-Brown formula.

parallel item in the Supervisory Behavior Description questionnaire. An ideal but time consuming procedure would have been to repeat the factor analysis on the *attitude* form but the independence of dimensions seems to have been established by the procedure employed. At least it appears that the usual "halo" effect, which often inflates the intercorrelation among keys in instruments of this type, has been efficiently partialed out in the revised form. The distributions of scores obtained for each of the questionnaire dimensions are roughly normal in shape.

The implication of these findings seems to be that the dimensions of "Consideration" and "Initiating Structure" are as meaningful and as independent in the attitudinal domain of leadership as in the behavioral realm. It thus appears that supervisors may be high in the amount of consideration they feel should be shown their subordinates, but at the same time may be either low or high in the amount of planning, criticizing, pushing for production, and general "structuring" behavior that they feel they should engage in.

INTERNAL CONSISTENCY RELIABILITY

Table 3 summarizes the available data on internal consistency reliabilities of the attitude scales on several samples. These reliabilities represent the correlation of odd numbered items with even numbered items corrected for full length of each scale by the Spearman-Brown formula. This table presents reliabilities for three

TABLE 3—Summary of Internal Consistency Reliabilities Obtained With the Leadership Opinion Questionnaire from Various Samples

N	Sample	Attitude Described	Dimension	
			Consideration	Initiating Structure
			r	r
122	Foremen	How I should lead my work group	.70	.79
394	Workers	How an ideal foreman should lead	.89	.88
60	General Foremen	How I should lead my foreman	.60	.82
60	General Foremen	How work groups should be led	.64	.78
202	ROTC Cadets	How I should lead	.82	.80

industrial samples at different levels in the plant as well as for a sample of ROTC cadets. Data on ROTC cadets was provided by Bass and Coates (2). The sample of workers filled out the form in terms of "how an ideal foreman should act." The ROTC group and foremen groups filled out the form in terms of their own leadership attitudes. The general foremen filled out forms on two separate occasions. In the first they answered in terms of how workers should be supervised and later in terms of how foremen should be supervised.

The reliabilities are generally maintained at an acceptable level across these samples. It is of interest to note that reliability suffered most when the general foremen filled out the form, and only in the case of the Consideration score. This was true for both administrations to the general foremen group.

TEST-RETEST RELIABILITIES

Table 4 summarizes data on test-retest reliabilities from two very different samples.

TABLE 4—Test-Retest Reliability Coefficients Obtained With the Leadership Opinion Questionnaire

N	Sample	Time Between Administrations	Dimension	
			Consideration	Initiating Structure
			r	r
31	Foremen	3 Months	.80	.74
24	Air Force NCO's	1 Month	.77	.67

It can be seen that adequate test-retest reliabilities were maintained for a sample of foremen with a 3-month period between administrations, as well as for a sample of Air Force NCO's with an interval of one month intervening. The data for NCO personnel were provided by DiVesta (4).

It should be added that the intervention of human relations training may considerably reduce the test-retest correlation (see 7, 11), as was the case with the Supervisory Behavior Description.

INTERCORRELATIONS BETWEEN THE SCALES

Table 5 summarizes the rather striking evidence regarding the independence of these scales in a variety of situations. The table summarizes data obtained from bakery supervisors, Naval officer candidates, Air Force noncommissioned officers, Army ROTC cadets, and samples of workers, foremen, and supervisors of foremen at the International Harvester Company. The data on naval officer candidates were provided by Glickman (8, 9). The median correlation between dimensions is $-.07$.

TABLE 5—Correlations Between Dimension Scores on the Leadership Opinion Questionnaire for Various Samples

N	Sample	r
122	Industrial Foremen	—.01
46	Industrial Foremen	—.07
202	ROTC Cadets	—.09
80	Bakery Supervisors	—.19
247	Naval Officer Candidates	—.23[a]
274	Naval Officer Candidates	—.21[a]
47	Air Force NCO's	.02
47	Air Force NCO's	.08
394	Industrial Workers	.04
60	General Foremen	—.23

[a] Significant at the .01 level of confidence.

It thus appears that supervisors may be high in the amount of consideration they feel should be shown their subordinates, but at the same time they may score either low or high in the amount of planning, criticizing, pushing for production, and general "Structuring" behavior that they feel they should engage in. Just as interesting is the indication that workers who want a great deal of "Consideration" in their foremen do not *necessarily* want less "Structuring" or more "Structuring" of their work activities from them. The only correlations between dimensions which reach statistical significance are those for the two separate samples of Naval officer candidates. Among these samples there is a slight tendency to associate high "Consideration" with low "Initiating Structure" attitudes.

VALIDITY OF THE QUESTIONNAIRE

As was the case with the Supervisory Behavior Description, another way of assessing the utility of the Leadership Opinion Questionnaire was in terms of correlations with independent measures of leadership effectiveness.

TABLE 6—Correlations Between the Leadership Opinion Questionnaire Dimensions and Various Criteria

Sample	N	Criterion	Dimension	
			Consideration	Initiating Structure
			r	r
ROTC Cadets	145	Merit ratings on campus by supervisors	—.21[a]	—.12
ROTC Cadets	71	Merit ratings in summer camp by supervisors	—.04	—.18
ROTC Cadets	200	Ratings by peers on campus	—.03	.03
ROTC Cadets	145	Situational Test (LDG)	—.18[b]	—.02
ROTC Cadets	189	Situational Test (LDG) in a later group	.03	.06
Foremen in chemical plant	53	Forced-choice performance ratings 2 years later	.29[b]	—.09
Navy OCS	116	Peer ratings	—.01	.03
Navy OCS	247	Peer ratings	—.02	—.08
Navy OCS	274	Academic Summer grades	.10	—.05
ROTC Cadets	145	3-year grade point average	—.13	—.04
ROTC Cadets	145	ACE Quantitative plus Language Score	—.16	—.13
Navy OCS	247	Navy Verbal Numerical Test	.04	.04
Navy OCS	274	Navy Verbal Numerical Test	.08	—.01
Navy OCS	247	Mid-term Academic average	.05	—.02
Bakery Supervisors	80	Wonderlic	.19	—.27[b]

[a] Significant at .01 level.
[b] Significant at .05 level.

Table 6 summarizes the data available from several sources. It can be seen that most of these correlations are essentially zero. A statistically significant, but low, negative correlation was obtained between Consideration scores of ROTC cadets and merit ratings given these cadets by superior officers. Similarly, a significant negative correlation was obtained by this ROTC sample with subsequent performance on a situational leadership test, represented by ratings of "amount of successful leadership displayed" in a Leaderless Group Discussion. However, even this low degree of relationship did not hold up for a second, later situational test. The scales were not predictive of peer ratings or academic grades among Naval officer candidates.

The one industrial criterion employed is worthy of note. The Leadership Opinion Questionnaire was administered to a sample of first line supervisors in a large petrochemical refinery. Two years later a carefully standardized forced choice performance report was administered to the supervisors of the respondents in the original sample. Over this lengthy period a significant correlation of .29 was achieved between the Consideration scale and the subsequent performance ratings. This study was performed by Bass (2).

It can be seen in Table 6 that scores achieved on the questionnaire are quite independent of the several measures of "intelligence" represented. No relationship was found between either "Consideration" or "Initiating Structure" and the 3-year grade point average or ACE examination scores of Army ROTC cadets. This is confirmed by the lack of relationship with essentially similar variables (academic average and verbal-numerical test score) among Naval officer candidates. In an industrial sample of bakery supervisors, the Wonderlic Group Test of Intelligence showed no significant correlation with Consideration attitudes, but there was a slight tendency for the supervisors scoring high in the Wonderlic test to score lower on Initiating Structure. This latter correlation of $-.27$ was low and the only statistically significant relationship found. The independence of these leadership attitude measures from traditional intelligence measures is in marked contrast to that reported for other leadership attitude questionnaires. For example, the File-Remmers, "How Supervise?" which probably has been the most widely used leadership attitude questionnaire, has been shown to reflect largely the intelligence of the respondent (13). The exclusion of intelligence variance from the leadership attitude measure represents a distinct methodological advance in this area of measurement.

Table 7 summarizes additional correlations with psychometric and other measures. Of interest in this table is the finding that the Leadership Opinion Questionnaire measures aspects of leadership

TABLE 7—Correlations of Leadership Opinion Questionnaire Dimensions and Various Psychometric and Other Measures

			Dimension	
Measure	Sample	N	Consideration	Initiating Structure
			r	r
Officer Qualification Test	Navy OCS	247	.06	—.13[b]
Officer Qualification Test	Navy OCS	274	.10	—.15
Naval Knowledge Test	Navy OCS	247	.05	—.05
Naval Knowledge Test	Navy OCS	274	.09	—.06
Level of Aspiration Score—Academic	Navy OCS	247	.02	—.09
Level of Aspiration Score—Academic	Navy OCS	274	.02	—.10
Level of Aspiration—Military	Navy OCS	247	—.14	.02
Level of Aspiration—Military	Navy OCS	274	—.14	.02
F Scale	Navy OCS	247	—.10	.15[b]
F Scale	Navy OCS	274	—.08	.17[a]
F Scale	Army ROTC	189	—.01	.12
Gestalt Completion	Army ROTC	98	.15	.07
Concealed Figures	Army ROTC	125	—.04	—.04
Empathy Test	Bakery Supervisors	80	.28[b]	—.04
Guilford-Holley Leadership Scales	Bakery Supervisors	80		
Benevolence			.33[a]	.01
Ambition			—.05	.28[a]
Meticulous			—.10	.37[a]
Discipline			—.21[b]	.35[a]
Aggression			—.15	.20
Guilford-Martin	Bakery Supervisors	80		
Objectivity			.07	—.02
Agreeable			.22[b]	—.20
Cooperative			.20	—.13
Johnson Temperament Schedule	Bakery Supervisors	64		
Composure			.28[b]	—.10
Gay Depressive			.07	.02
Activity			—.09	—.12
Cordiality			.12	.15
Sympathetic			.10	.01
Objectivity			—.04	.03
Aggression			—.10	.10
Critical			.04	.26[b]
Self-Mastery			—.05	.05
Bernreuter	Bakery Supervisors	64		
Emotional Adjustment			.10	—.21
Self Sufficiency			.09	—.06
Dominance			.03	.12
Socialness			.16	.33[a]

[a] Significant at the .01 level.
[b] Significant at the .05 level.

attitudes quite independent of whatever leadership "qualities" are measured by the Navy Officer Qualification test. For each of two independent samples of Naval OCS students Consideration attitudes showed no relationship, but attitudes toward Initiating Structure showed a low, although significant, negative correlation with the Officer Qualification Test. No significant correlations were found between Naval Knowledge Test scores or perceptual closure as measured by the Gestalt Completion and Concealed Figure Tests.

The remaining variables in Table 7 represent measures of different aspects of "personality." No relationship was found between these scales and level of aspiration, military or academic, whether self ascribed or ascribed by peers. Of interest is the finding that scores on the F scale measure of authoritarianism (1) did not correlate with the Consideration scale in either the sample of Naval OCS students or in the case of Army ROTC students. However, a low but significantly positive correlation was obtained in two Navy samples between Initiating Structure and scores on the F scale. A correlation of the same magnitude was obtained in the ROTC sample, although this latter coefficient, based on a smaller N, is not statistically significant.

There has been considerable interest in the literature concerning the Empathy Test developed by Kerr and Speroff (12). The test which purports to measure the ability of an individual "to put himself in someone else's place" has been seen of special relevance to problems of leadership. Results in a large bakery with the Leadership Opinion Questionnaire do yield a significant correlation of .28 with Consideration which makes some psychological sense. No correlation was found with Initiating Structure.

The remaining correlations were also obtained with the bakery sample of supervisors and represent relationships with certain standard personality questionnaires. No extensive interpretation of these correlations will be attempted in view of the well-known limitations of such questionnaire scores. It is to be stressed that the labels given questionnaire "scales" may not correspond to the trait measured, and several scales with the same name may actually be measuring different things. However, the significant correlations obtained generally are consistent with what one would expect, although the absence of correlation in some cases is not readily explainable. Thus, supervisors high in Consideration score high in "benevolence" and low in "discipline," and supervisors high in Structure attitudes score high in ambition, meticulousness, and discipline on the Guilford-

Holley Leadership Inventory. In general, the correlations between leadership attitudes and personality measures of this type are low or insignificant.

NORMATIVE DATA

Table 8 summarizes the means and standard deviations obtained with the questionnaire in various samples. While not substitutes for complete norms based on larger samples, these data offer at least a rough basis for comparative purposes.

TABLE 8—Means and Standard Deviations of Leadership Opinion Questionnaire Scores for Various Samples

N	Sample	Attitude Described	Dimension			
			Consideration		Initiating Structure	
			M	SD	M	SD
122	Foremen	How I should lead my work group	53.9	7.2	53.3	7.8
31	Foremen	How I should lead my work group	54.1	6.6	52.9	6.1
31	Foremen	How I should lead my work group	56.0	8.1	52.6	9.1
46	Foremen	How I should lead my work group	54.7	7.7	54.4	5.6
394	Workers	How an ideal foreman should lead	57.0	5.5	44.2	3.9
60	General Foremen	How I should lead my foremen	58.0	6.4	52.4	7.6
60	General Foremen	How work groups should be led	53.0	7.3	54.0	6.7
80	Bakery Supervisors	How I should lead my workers	62.1	7.1	48.9	8.5
274	Navy OCS	How I should lead	44.2	8.5	55.4	7.0
24	Air Force NCO's	How I should lead	58.0	7.0	52.0	7.7
94	Air Force NCO's	How I should lead	56.3	8.0	54.8	7.3

Table 8 shows that the means of each of the 4 foremen groups are in the same general range within each scale. These foremen groups scored considerably lower than the bakery first-line supervisors and somewhat lower, on the average, than Air Force noncommissioned officers on the "Consideration" key. Another comparison shows that General Foremen tend to be more "Considerate" in their leadership attitudes toward foremen than toward workers. Perhaps, the most interesting comparison shows that supervisors in the bakery sample scored higher on "Consideration" than did the sample of *workers* in the International Harvester plant. These workers filled out the form in terms of "how an ideal foreman should act." This may be a further suggestion of the importance of "leadership climate" in determining leadership attitudes at all levels in an organization. Other factors, such as type of work, may also be contributing. The important point made is that these scales are sensitive in revealing differences between different work situations.

On the "Initiating Structure" key differences in the samples were not as marked. The industrial foremen, general foremen, and Air Force NCO's and Navy OCS cadets score about the same. However, the worker sample scored significantly lower in the amount of "structure" desired than did the other samples. Also, bakery supervisors feel that less structure should be initiated when compared to other supervisory groups. This, of course, may reflect the nature of the work or other factors.

SUMMARY

This section has summarized the evidence available on the Leadership Opinion Questionnaire, a measure of leadership attitudes parallel to the Supervisory Behavior Description described in the preceding section. Its development from previous research, its construction, revision, and standardization on industrial samples were described as well as its subsequent evaluations in a variety of situations. Like the final forms of the Air Force Leader Behavior Description and the Industrial Supervisory Behavior Description, the Leadership Opinion Questionnaire is designed to provide independent measures of "Consideration" and "Initiating Structure."

These scales were shown to be reliable and independent in a wide variety of situations. Internal consistency as well as test-retest reliability was assessed. Validity was evaluated through correlations with independent leadership measures, such as merit rating by supervisors, peer ratings, forced-choice performance reports by management, and leaderless group situation tests. Relatively low validities were found for the particular criteria employed, although a few statistically significant correlations were found. The need for validation against more industrial criteria was indicated. Correlations with other measures revealed that scores on the Leadership Opinion Questionnaire were independent of the "intelligence" of the supervisor, an advantage not achieved by other available leadership attitude questionnaires. Generally low to insignificant correlations were obtained between the questionnaire scales and questionnaire measures of personality, although the few significant correlations found were psychologically meaningful.

The questionnaire scores have been found to be sensitive for discriminating reliably between leadership attitudes in different situations as well as for evaluating the effects of leadership training. While not considered a substitute for the Supervisory Behavior Description, the evidence indicates that the Leadership Opinion Questionnaire can be valuable in a variety of leadership-group situations where primary concern is in the assessment of leadership attitudes.

References

1. Adorno, T. W., Frenkel-Brunswick, E., et al. *The Authoritarian Personality.* New York: Harpers, 1950.
2. Bass, B. M. Leadership Opinions as Forecasts of Supervisory Success. Unpublished manuscript.
3. Bass, B. M., and Coates, C. H. Situational and Personality Factors in Leadership in ROTC. Unpublished manuscript, L.S.U.
4. Di Vesta, F. J. Instructor-Centered and Student-Centered Approaches in Teaching a Human Relations Course. *J. Appl. Psychol.*, 1954, *38*, 329–335.
5. Fleishman, E. A. The Measurement of Leadership Attitudes in Industry. *J. Appl. Psychol.*, 1953, *36*, 153–158.
6. Fleishman, E. A. Leadership Climate, Human Relations Training, and Supervisory Behavior. *Personnel Psychol.*, 1953, *6*, 205–222.
7. Fleishman, E. A., Harris, E. F., and Burtt, H. E. *Leadership and Supervision in Industry.* Columbus, Ohio: Bureau of Educational Research, Ohio State University, 1955.
8. Glickman, A. S. Development and Validation of a Battery to Predict Peer Ratings of Navy Officer Candidates. *BuPers. Tech. Bull.*, No. 54–13, 1954.
9. Glickman, A. S., and Vallance, T. R. Development and Validation of an Experimental Battery to Select Officer Candidates for the Navy. *BuPers. Tech. Bull.*, No. 54–12, 1954.
10. Halpin, A. W. The Leadership Ideology of Aircraft Commanders. *J. Appl. Psychol.*, 1954, *38*, 329–334.
11. Harris, E. F., and Fleishman, E. A. Human Relations Training and the Stability of Leadership Patterns. *J. Appl. Psychology.*, 1955, *39*, 20–25.
12. Kerr, W. A., and Speroff, B. J. The Measurement of Empathy. *Psychometric Affiliates*, 1951.
13. Weitz, J., and Nuckols, R. C. A Validation Study of "How Supervise?" *J. Appl. Psychol.*, 1953, *37*, 7–8.

XI

LEADERSHIP OPINIONS AND RELATED CHARACTERISTICS OF SALESMEN AND SALES MANAGERS

BERNARD M. BASS
Louisiana State University

As part of a test validation project, the Leader Behavior Description Questionnaire (LBDQ) was administered to 265 salesmen and sales supervisors of a foods distributing company.

SAMPLE AND MEASURES

Sample—For purposes of cross-validation, six samples were organized. The number of salesmen and supervisors in each sample, and the parts of the country in which they were working were as follows:

- A 62 salesmen from the North, Midwest or West.
- B 66 salesmen from the North, Midwest or West.
- C 33 salesmen from the South including Texas and Oklahoma.
- D 42 salesmen from the South including Texas and Oklahoma.
- E 34 nationally distributed sales supervisors.
- F 28 nationally distributed sales supervisors.

Personal Characteristics—Scores on the following personal characteristics were available on each salesman and supervisor:

- P 1. Years with the company (seniority).
- P 2. Years of education.
- P 3. Marital status.
- P 4. Age when tested.

Ratings—The following ratings of examinees by superiors and associates were available:

- R 1. *Visibility*. The number of associates in an examinee's division who knew him by name, at least.

RELATED CHARACTERISTICS

R 2. *Popularity*. The percentage of associates who knew him, and who nominated rather than rejected the examinee as one with whom they would like to work.
R 3. *Esteem*. Similar nomination as "of value to the company."
R 4. *Ability*. Similar nomination as "able to solve problems of the job."
R 5. *Influence*. Similar nomination as "able to influence the rater."
R 6. *Merit*. Average merit score assigned by immediate superior and his boss using a 20-item discriminate binary check list.

Tests—The following tests were administered to each examinee along with the LBDQ:

T 1. Wonderlic Personnel Test, Form D.
T 2. Gestalt Completion (a mutilated figures test developed by L. L. Thurstone aimed at measuring perceptual flexibility).
T 3. Concealed Figures (a similar type hidden pattern test).
T 4. Kerr Empathy Test (Form B).
T 5. Bruce Business Judgment Test (human relations multiple choice questions).
T 6. Bruce Sales Knowledge Test (merchandising, advertising and marketing multiple choice questions).
T 7. Bruce Sales Interest (Items similar to the Strong Vocational Interest Inventory).
T 8. How Supervise.
T 9. Famous Sayings—Conventional Mores.
T 10. —Hostility.
T 11. —Fear of Failure.
T 12. —Social Acquiescence.
T 13. Gordon Personal Profile—Ascendency.
T 14. —Responsibility.
T 15. —Emotional Stability.
T 16. —Sociability.

RESULTS

Table 1 shows the means and standard deviations of scores on Initiation and Consideration for the 6 samples. Inspection of Table 1 suggests that sales supervisors consistently favored both more consideration and more initiation than did salesmen, although the differences are probably too small to attain statistical significance. A

TABLE 1—Leader Behavior Scores Correlated With Personal Characteristics and Performance Ratings

	Initiation: Samples A to F						Consideration: Samples A to F					
	A	B	C	D	E	F	A	B	C	D	E	F
	r	r	r	r	r	r	r	r	r	r	r	r
Personal												
Seniority	03	−10	02	07	−18	06	−10	18	−03	09	26	35
Education	06	20	−29	04	06	02	−11	−02	15	−16	03	−24
Marriage	−15	−15	02	−06	−32	00	10	−06	01	03	−12	00
Age	13	−21	02	15	−30	21	−03	18	−18	19	28	30
Rating												
Visibility	20	−13	07	09	−11	25	−09	10	−29	−02	−04	−03
Popularity	−05	04	05	07	12	−04	04	13	04	−17	06	−09
Esteem	04	15	03	08	10	−09	−05	−03	−21	−21	08	−11
Ability	16	−05	−02	−07	−06	14	04	16	−19	00	05	00
Influence	10	−06	−07	02	15	15	11	16	−20	−03	−18	−09
Merit	−18	15	−01	01	−05	15	08	09	−03	−18	−02	02
Number	62	63	33	42	34	28	62	63	33	42	34	28
Mean	59.0	58.8	58.2	57.6	60.3	60.3	54.3	55.6	57.5	56.9	57.8	58.0
S.D.	7.9	7.2	6.9	7.4	5.6	6.5	7.8	7.8	9.1	6.0	8.5	6.4

Note: Decimal points omitted.

slight regional interaction also appeared. The two samples of Southern salesmen favored more Consideration and less Initiation than did the other two samples of fellow salesmen.

Table 1 also shows the correlations between the Leader Behavior scores and personal characteristics. Consideration is positively correlated with age and seniority in both supervisor samples. The correlations, which are close to .30, approach statistical significance. Age and marital status are negatively related to Initiation in supervisor sample E. None of the personal characteristics is highly correlated with the leader behavior scores of salesmen. It may be seen in Table 1 that none of the ratings by superiors and subordinates is related to the leader behavior description scores for salesmen or supervisors.

The correlations between the leader behavior scores and various tests and inventories are shown in Table 2. Initiation is positively correlated with sales interest and ascendency in all samples. Sales knowledge and emotional stability are positively related to Initiation for all samples, except supervisory sample E. Business judgment is negatively correlated with Initiation in the two salesmen samples C and D, while fear of failure is positively related to Initiation in salesmen samples A and B. Responsibility is positively related to Initiation for salesmen, but negatively for supervisors. Apparently the assumption of responsibility involves a greater degree of initiating structure in selling than it does in supervising.

Consideration is positively correlated with the How Supervise test in all samples. Consideration scores are also positively related to acquiescence and conventional mores in samples C and D. However, Consideration is correlated negatively with the Gestalt Completion test and with ascendency in most samples.

SUMMARY

The Leader Behavior Description Questionnaire and a large battery of other tests were administered to 4 samples of salesmen and two samples of supervisors. Supervisors endorsed a higher degree of Consideration and Initiation than did salesmen. Supervisors who are older and have been longer with the company score higher on Consideration. Initiation is positively related to sales interest and

TABLE 2—Correlations Between Leadership Dimension Scores and Psychological Test Scores

Psychological Test	Initiation: Samples A to F						Consideration: Samples A to F					
	A	B	C	D	E	F	A	B	C	D	E	F
	r	r	r	r	r	r	r	r	r	r	r	r
T1 Wonderlic	−19	15	14	05	−19	34	23	01	09	00	35	15
T2 Gestalt Completion	−02	18	22	02	01	−10	−04	−12	−17	−02	−24	−06
T3 Concealed Figures	00	11	18	−29	−26	24	03	06	−01	10	38	−35
T4 Kerr Empathy	−01	09	−28	06	02	10	−18	−05	28	04	−15	08
T5 Business Judgment	00	−02	−24	−44	13	−01	05	01	−12	20	25	06
T6 Sales Knowledge	13	33	19	32	−23	24	−19	17	09	−09	18	−08
T7 Sales Interest	19	39	34	11	15	30	06	12	−02	04	−13	−34
T8 How Supervise	−09	12	−05	11	−02	24	27	32	23	28	34	03
T9 Conventional Mores	−15	08	−18	−09	31	06	−10	03	16	25	02	36
T10 Hostility	00	13	−02	−10	−24	11	07	−05	07	−03	−14	13
T11 Fear Failure	25	29	−04	06	−02	29	−01	01	48	−02	07	31
T12 Acquiescence	−03	20	−18	01	12	24	21	−03	32	32	06	27
T13 Ascendancy	11	29	34	29	44	33	02	−06	−27	−24	−24	−18
T14 Responsibility	33	22	17	20	−22	−19	−19	23	−28	25	31	−11
T15 Emotional Stability	14	17	10	22	−20	10	02	03	−18	00	24	−09
T16 Sociability	−03	08	28	04	36	00	14	02	00	13	−16	07

Note: All decimal points omitted.

ascendency in all samples. Consideration is positively related to scores on the How Supervise test on all samples. Responsibility is positively correlated with Initiation for salesmen, but negatively for supervisors. Some regional differences are also noted.

References

1. Bass, B. M. Development and Evaluation of a Scale for Measuring Social Acquiescence. *J. Abnorm. Soc. Psychol.*, 1956, *53*, 296–299.
2. Bass, B. M. Development of a Structured Disguised Personality Inventory. *J. Appl. Psychol.*, 1956, *40*, 393–397.
3. Bass, B. M. Reducing Leniency in Merit Ratings. *Personnel Psychol.*, 1956, *9*, 359–369.

XII

A FACTORIAL STUDY OF VERY SHORT SCALES[1]

RALPH M. STOGDILL, *The Ohio State University*
ELLIS L. SCOTT, *The Rand Corporation*
and
WILLIAM E. JAYNES, *U.S. Army Medical Research Laboratory*

When busy subjects are able to spare only a limited amount of time for filling out questionnaires, it is necessary for the experimenter to decide whether he wishes to measure a small number of variables with a high degree of reliability, or a large number of variables with a lesser degree of reliability. The design for the Studies on Naval Leadership required the investigation of a large number of variables. It was decided to employ short scales in order to obtain data on several sets of variables rather than to strive for maximum reliability.

The results obtained with a set of short scales have been decribed by Stogdill and Shartle (3), Scott (2), Campbell (1), and Stogdill, Scott and Jaynes (5). The hypothetical dimensions used in these studies, and the number of items in the scales for each dimension were as follows: Communication (6 items), Representation (4 items), Organization (4 items), Integration (4 items), Cordial Relations with Subordinates (2 items), and Cordial Relations with Superiors (2 items). All the items, except those for cordial relations with superiors and subordinates, were drawn from the battery of 150 items described in Section II of this monograph.

Stogdill and Shartle (3) report odd-even reliabilities ranging from .31 to .76 for the separate scales when used for self-descriptions, and a reliability of .93 for the total score based on the sum of the 22 items. The reliabilities for descriptions by other persons range from .51 to .85 for the separate scales. The reliability of the total score is .89. Test-retest reliabilities range from .52 to .79 for the separate

---

[1] This study was sponsored cooperatively by the Office of Naval Research and The Ohio State University Research Foundation.

scales, with a reliability of .82 for the total score. These reliabilities are as high as could be expected with scales composed of 2 to 6 items.

The dimension (scale) scores were intercorrelated for numerous samples of subjects (1,2,3,4,5). Both self-descriptions and descriptions by other persons are rather highly intercorrelated.

LEADER BEHAVIOR DESCRIPTIONS INTERCORRELATED

The intercorrelations for several samples of subjects were factor analyzed. In Table 1 are shown the intercorrelations among the self-description scores of 42 commissioned officers on a cruiser. Table 2 shows the correlations for the self-description scores of 33 officers in a naval command staff.

TABLE 1—Intercorrelations Among Leader Behavior Dimension Scores of 42 Officers on a Cruiser

Leader Behavior Dimension	Leader Behavior Dimension					
	1	2	3	4	5	6
	r	r	r	r	r	r
1. Integration		.61	.60	.57	.60	.12
2. Relation to Superiors	.61		.72	.44	.43	.13
3. Relation to Subordinates	.60	.72		.42	.43	.13
4. Communication	.57	.44	.42		.56	.01
5. Organization	.60	.43	.43	.56		—.06
6. Representation	.12	.13	.13	.01	—.06	

TABLE 2—Intercorrelations Among Leader Behavior Dimension Scores of 33 Officers in a Naval Command Staff

Leader Behavior Dimension	Leader Behavior Dimension					
	1	2	3	4	5	6
	r	r	r	r	r	r
1. Integration		.34	.17	.78	.50	.41
2. Relation to Superiors	.34		.83	.19	.28	.25
3. Relation to Subordinates	.17	.83		.16	.33	.08
4. Communication	.78	.19	.16		.56	.10
5. Organization	.50	.28	.33	.56		.37
6. Representation	.41	.25	.08	.10	.37	

Factor analysis resulted in the identification of three orthogonal factors for each of the two tables of intercorrelations. The factors were rotated to maximize meaningfulness as well as comparability between the two samples. The final rotated factor loadings are shown in Table 3.

Factor I has its highest loadings in both samples on Integration, Communication and Organization. In the cruiser, rather high loadings are also shown on Cordial Relations with Superiors and Cordial Relations with Subordinates. Considering the nature of the organizations from which these data were derived, this factor might be identified as *Administrative Control*. This factor appears to have much in common with the factor identified by Hemphill and others as "Initiation of Structure in Interaction."

Factor II shows high loadings only on Cordial Relations with Superiors and Cordial Relations with Subordinates. This factor is therefore, identified as *Effective Interpersonal Relations*. This factor would appear to parallel that identified by Hemphill and others

TABLE 3—Factor Loadings Derived From Analysis of Tables 1 and 2

Leader Behavior Dimension	Cruiser Factor			Command Staff Factor		
	I	II	III	I	II	III
1. Integration	.83	.15	.19	.91	.03	.25
2. Communication	.76	—.15	.10	.90	.02	.00
3. Organization	.75	—.07	—.18	.54	.16	.39
4. Relation to Superiors	.65	.52	.13	.29	.88	.15
5. Relation to Subordinates	.63	.54	.09	.20	.87	.13
6. Representation	.02	.15	.44	.19	.06	.64

as "Consideration." However, due to differences in the content of the items, Factor II cannot be regarded as identical with the Consideration factor.

Factor III has its highest loading on Representation, with only moderately high loadings on Integration and Organization in the command staff. The factor is therefore identified as *Public Relations* or *Representation*. The emergence of this factor differs from the results obtained in other studies reported in this monograph. Its appearance in both command staffs and cruisers lends weight to the reality of the factor. Its appearance in the Navy organizations and its absence in other groups studied is probably due to differences in the samples. The Navy samples represent large, structured organizations with clearly defined and differentiated administrative functions carried out by top level personnel. In contrast, the leaders of air crews, foremen samples and miscellaneous groups represent types of leadership involving face-to-face interaction and the direction of first line operations. Public Relations functions are usually located in higher level administrative positions.

LEADER BEHAVIOR DESCRIPTIONS CORRELATED WITH OTHER VARIABLES

In two additional samples, the leader behavior description scores were correlated with other variables. The subjects were 48 commissioned officers in landing ships (LST), and 57 military and civilian administrators in a naval research organization. The descriptions were made by the immediate subordinates of the subjects.

The variables correlated with the leader behavior descriptions include Level and Military Rank (measures of vertical status), Sociometric Score (number of mentions received as work partner), Time in Job, Ratings for Leader Effectiveness by Superiors, and Responsibility, Authority, and Delegation self-descriptions. The intercorrelations are shown in Tables 4 and 5. It will be noted that level and

TABLE 4—Intercorrelations Among Leadership Measures in a Research Organization

Variables	Variables											
	1	2	3	4	5	6	7	8	9	10	11	12
	r	r	r	r	r	r	r	r	r	r	r	r
1. Level		76	38	—08	14	38	27	06	—12	—20	—13	—01
2. Military Rank	76		25	04	15	33	29	08	—18	—24	—20	—22
3. Sociometric Score	38	25		—29	20	—24	—15	—08	04	05	03	19
4. Time in Position	—08	04	—29		—01	39	15	04	—07	—19	—21	—09
5. Leadership Rating	14	15	20	—01		—08	07	—22	07	21	05	07
6. Responsibility	38	33	—24	39	—08		59	28	—22	—21	—09	—22
7. Authority	27	29	—15	15	07	59		32	—13	13	30	07
8. Delegation	06	08	—08	04	—22	28	32		26	23	12	—06
9. Organization	—12	—18	04	—07	07	—22	—13	26		63	43	31
10. Integration	—20	—24	05	—19	21	—21	13	23	63		78	36
11. Juniors	—13	—20	03	—21	05	—09	30	12	43	78		45
12. Seniors	—01	—22	19	—09	07	—22	07	—06	31	36	45	

Note: All decimal points omitted.
N = 57 Military and civilian administrators.

rank are highly correlated, as are the leader behavior descriptions by subordinates (variables 9–14). Responsibility (variable 6) and Authority (variable 7) are also fairly highly related in both tables.

The results of the factor analysis of the data in Tables 4 and 5

144 LEADER BEHAVIOR: ITS DESCRIPTION AND MEASUREMENT

TABLE 5—Intercorrelations Among Leadership Measures in Landing Ships (LST)

Variables	1	2	4	5	6	7	8	9	10	11	12	13	14
	r	r	r	r	r	r	r	r	r	r	r	r	r
1. Level		78	−05	16	04	22	33	−21	−07	−05	01	−05	−06
2. Military Rank	78		16	33	11	11	31	−07	01	06	01	07	07
4. Time in Position	−05	16		35	01	00	−11	−01	−31	−12	−30	−18	22
5. Leadership Rating	16	33	35		02	24	−01	02	−08	02	−14	−02	30
6. Responsibility	04	11	01	02		57	09	−04	06	19	12	03	06
7. Authority	22	11	00	24	57		21	09	22	20	23	11	22
8. Delegation	33	31	−11	−01	09	21		18	31	17	10	12	−08
9. Organization	−21	−07	−01	02	−04	09	18		50	45	69	70	17
10. Integration	−07	01	−31	−08	06	22	31	50		50	54	52	26
11. Relation to Juniors	−05	06	−12	02	19	20	17	45	50		46	58	39
12. Relation to Seniors	01	01	−30	−14	12	23	10	69	54	46		50	−05
13. Communication	−05	07	−18	−02	03	11	12	70	52	58	50		35
14. Representation	−06	07	22	30	06	22	−08	17	26	39	−05	35	

Note: All decimal points omitted.
N = 48 Commissioned officers.

TABLE 6—Final Rotated Factor Loadings for Two Samples: LST's and Research Organizations

Variables	I		II		III		IV		V		VI
	LST	Research	LST	Research	LST	Research	LST	Research	LST	Research	LST
					Factor Loadings						
1. Level	74	86	41	41	03	−13	−13	−19	−18	00	−05
2. Rank	81	70	32	48	06	−19	15	−02	05	−05	05
3. Sociometric Score		52		−19		06		−15		10	
4. Time on Job	12	−19	28		−13	−19	52	43	−19	−15	05
5. Leadership Rating	27	40	11	−07	−05	20	54	30	05	00	17
6. Responsibility	−19	02	62	77	06	−08	07	12	−12	−19	08
7. Authority	−12	−02	76	75	10	32	−17	−10	18	−12	05
8. Delegation	33	−18	27	40	11	−03	−17	−13	42	47	−06
9. Organization	−12	−07	−13	−19	72	30	19	19	42	68	05
10. Integration	−04	−16	18	−08	46	77	−13	06	46	45	32
11. Relation to Juniors	−05	−15	14	−03	54	82	04	−18	13	28	51
12. Relation to Seniors	−19	05	15	−19	82	51	−15	−01	16	11	−16
13. Communication	−02		−05		74		00		13		33
14. Representation	−01		04		12		36		05		58

Note: All decimal points omitted.

are shown in Table 6. Five orthogonal factors emerged in the analysis of Table 4 for the research organization, while 6 factors were found to account for the variance in Table 5 for landing ships. The factors were rotated to maximize meaningfulness as well as comparability between the two organizations.

Factor I has its high loadings on variables 1, 2, 3 and 5. These are Level, Rank, Sociometric Score, and Leadership Rating. The highest loadings are on Level and Rank. Sociometric Score, available only for the research organization, shows a high loading only on Factor I. Leadership Effectiveness Rating shows somewhat higher loadings on another factor. These variables appear to be measuring high, formal leadership status. Factor I is identified as *Status in Organization*.

Factor II is shown to have high loadings on Responsibility and Authority, with moderately high loadings on Level, Rank, and Delegation. Responsibility shows high loadings only on this factor. This fact, along with the high loadings on Authority, Level and Rank, suggest the identification of this factor as *Responsibility*.

Factor III appears with high loadings on the leader behavior description variables: Organization, Integration, Cordial Relations with Juniors (Subordinates), Cordial Relations with Seniors (Superiors), and Communication. In the research organization, moderately high loadings are found also on Leadership Ratings and Authority. The nature of these items suggest that the factor may be identified as *Administrative Control*.

For Factor IV the highest loadings are obtained on variables 4, 5 and 14. These are Time in Position, Leadership Effectiveness Rating, and Representation. Organizing behavior (variable 9) is also measured to a small extent by this factor. The high loading on length of time in position, in conjunction with an absence of loading on high formal status, suggest the identification of this factor as *Established Position*. The loadings on effectiveness ratings by superiors and the descriptions of representing behavior by subordinates lend further weight to this interpretation.

The variables with high loadings on Factor V are Delegation, Organization and Integration. Cordial Relations with Subordinates also shows moderately high loadings on this factor. Level and Rank show low or negative weightings. The behavior described by this factor may be exhibited at any level in the administrative hierarchy.

The high loadings on Delegation, Organization, and Integration suggest the identification of the factor as *The Facilitation of Within —Group Interaction*. It is interesting to observe that Delegation obtains its highest loading on this factor. Ordinarily, the delegation of authority is considered in terms of executive efficiency and manageable work loads. In the present analysis, delegation (granting freedom to act) is found to play its leading role as a measure of group integration and freedom of action.

Factor VI, which appears only in the landing ship (LST) sample, shows its highest loadings on variables 14 and 11. These are Representation and Cordial Relations with Juniors. Communication and Integration (variables 13 and 10) show moderately high loadings on this factor, while variable 12 (Cordial Relations with Seniors) shows a negative weighting. The leader behaviors measured by this factor are clearly oriented toward subordinates. It is identified as the *Representation of Group Interests*. Leadership Effectiveness Rating also contributes a small amount to the measurement of this factor.

The fact that these factors appear in two separate samples constitutes a cross validation of the findings. About the only thing the two samples have in common is the fact that they are both naval organizations. The LST sample consists of the commanding officer, executive officer, and 2 or 3 subordinate officers from each of 10 landing ships. The research sample consists of both military and civilian personnel in a large organization containing many departments and subdivisions. The subjects represent 7 different echelons in the chain of command.

The leader behavior description scales were found to contribute to the measurement of more than one factor. Organizing and integrating behaviors (variables 9 and 10) contribute to Factors III and V (Administrative Control and Group Interaction Facilitation). Cordial Relations with Subordinates (variable 11) shows weightings on Factors III and VI, with a moderately high loading on Factor V for the research sample. Factor VI is the Representation of Group Interests. Cordial Relations with Seniors shows high loadings only on Factor III. Communication appears with loadings on Factors III and VI, while Representation shows high loadings only on Factors IV (Established Position) and VI (Representation of Group Interest). Again, Representation is shown to measure something apart from the behaviors measured by the other leader behavior description scales.

Level and Rank appear with high loadings on Factors I and II, while Sociometric Score contributes to the measurement of Factor I only. The Leadership Effectiveness Rating (variable 5) makes its primary contribution in the measurement of Factor I (Formal Status) and Factor IV (Established Position), with some suggestion of contribution to Factors III and VI.

Responsibility and Authority (variables 6 and 7) are the best measures of Factor II (Responsibility). Authority, however, makes a slight contribution to the measurement of Factors III, IV and V. Delegation emerges as a measure of Factor V (Facilitation of Interaction), Factor II (Responsibility), and Factor I (Formal Status).

SUMMARY AND DISCUSSION

A factor analysis of the intercorrelations among 6 short scales for the description of leader behavior resulted in the identification of 3 factors. The first, Administrative Control, appears to parallel a factor which other workers have identified as the "Initiation of Structure in Interaction." The second, Effective Interpersonal Relations, bears some resemblance to a factor identified by other workers as "Consideration." The third, Public Relations or Representation, emerges as a clearly differentiated behavior among high level administrators in structured organizations. The fact that these factors appear in two different samples (a cruiser and a command staff) lends credance to the results.

The leader behavior descriptions were also intercorrelated with other measures of leader behavior, status and effectiveness. A factor analysis of the tables of intercorrelations resulted in the emergence of 5 factors in one sample, and 6 factors in another. Five of the factors appeared with approximately identical loadings on the variables that measure the respective factors in the two different samples.

Two of the factors (Administrative Control and Representation of Group Interests) appeared in the analysis of the intercorrelations among the leader behavior description scores alone. One factor (Effective Interpersonal Relations) which appeared in the factor analysis of the leader behavior descriptions alone, did not appear when the leader behavior descriptions were correlated with other variables. This result appears to be due to the fact that the leader behavior descriptions contributed differentially to the measurement of Factors III, V and VI when correlated with other measures. Factor V (Interaction Facilitation) is not similar to the Effective Interpersonal Relations factor measured by the leader behavior descriptions alone.

This analysis shows the leader behavior descriptions to be relatively independent of formal status. All, except Representation and Organization are also independent of established position.

Leader behavior described by subordinates and self-descriptions of authority and delegation combine to measure the same dimensions, as represented by Factors III and V. The emergence of Delegation as a measure of group integrity and freedom of action must be regarded as one of the significant findings of the analysis.

The fact that the dimensions, *Administrative Control* and *Representation of Group Interests,* appear in four different organizations constitutes a cross validation of these factors in Navy organizations. Although the contents of these dimensions do not exactly parallel the content of the Consideration and Initiating Structure dimensions, there is a high degree of similarity between them.

REFERENCES

1. Campbell, Donald T. *Leader Behavior and Its Effects upon the Group.* Columbus: Ohio State University, Bureau of Business Research Monograph No. 83, 1956.
2. Scott, Ellis L. *Leadership and Perceptions of Organization,* Columbus: Ohio State University, Bureau of Business Research Monograph No. 82, 1956.
3. Stogdill, Ralph M. and Shartle, Carroll L., *Methods in the Study of Administrative Leadership.* Columbus: Ohio State University, Bureau of Business Research Monograph No. 80, 1955.
4. Stogdill, Ralph M., Shartle, Carroll L. and Associates, *Patterns of Administrative Performance.* Columbus: Ohio State University, Bureau of Business Research Monograph No. 81, 1956.
5. Stogdill, Ralph M., Scott, Ellis L. and Jaynes, William E., *Leadership and Role Expectations.* Columbus: Ohio State University, Bureau of Business Research Monograph No. 86, 1956.

APPENDIX A
LIST OF ITEMS IN THE
LEADER BEHAVIOR DESCRIPTION QUESTIONNAIRE
Original Form of 150 Items

APPENDIX A

List of Items
in the
Leader Behavior Description Questionnaire
(Original Form of 150 Items)

1. He plans his day's activities in detail.
2. He refuses to compromise a point.
3. He makes his attitudes clear to the group.
4. He does personal favors for group members.
5. He encourages the members to work as a team.
6. He expresses appreciation when a member does a good job.
7. He defends the group against criticism.
8. He encourages overtime work.
9. He tries out his new ideas in the group.
10. He has everything going according to schedule.
11. He rules with an iron hand.
12. He seeks information from group members.
13. He invites members to his home.
14. He does little things to make it pleasant to be a member of the group.
15. He criticizes poor work.
16. He makes outside contacts for the group.
17. He talks about how much should be done.
18. He stresses the need for new practices.
19. He meets with the group at regularly scheduled times.
20. He speaks in a manner not to be questioned.
21. He is easy to understand.
22. He engages in friendly jokes and comments during group meetings.
23. He sides with the same members in cases of disagreement.
24. He compliments a member on his work in front of others.
25. He sells the public on the importance of his group.
26. He asks for more than the members can get done.
27. He follows routine to the letter.
28. He works without a plan.
29. He uses his veto powers.
30. He keeps informed about the work that is being done.
31. He helps members of the group with their personal problems.
32. He helps new members make adjustments.
33. He criticizes a member in front of others.
34. He stands up for the group even if it makes him unpopular.
35. He encourages slow working members to greater effort.

36 He waits for the group to push new ideas.
37 He assigns members to particular tasks.
38 He insists that everything be done his way.
39 He keeps the group informed.
40 He works right along with the group.

41 He asks for sacrifices from individuals for the good of the group.
42 He sees that a member is rewarded for a job well done.
43 He speaks in public in the name of the group.
44 He sets an example by working hard himself.
45 He pushes new ways of doing things.

46 He asks that members follow organizational lines.
47 He yields to others in a discussion.
48 He finds time to listen to other members.
49 He asks to be called by his first name.
50 He encourages the group to organize social activities.

51 He criticizes members for small mistakes.
52 He seeks special advantages for his group.
53 He sees to it that members are working up to capacity.
54 He rejects suggestions for change.
55 He figures ahead on what should be done.

56 He has members share in making decisions.
57 He calls the group together to talk things over.
58 He discusses his personal problems with group members.
59 He encourages understanding of points of view of other members.
60 He reacts favorably to anything members do.

61 He takes the blame when outsiders criticize the group.
62 He emphasizes the quantity of work.
63 He changes his approach to meet new situations.
64 He maintains definite standards of performance.
65 He changes the duties of members without first talking it over with them.

66 He keeps well informed about the progress of the group.
67 He keeps to himself.
68 He gives personal attention to members who seem neglected.
69 He criticizes his own performance.
70 He is spokesman for the group.

71 He lets members work at their own speed.
72 He suggests new approaches to problems.
73 He treats members like cogs in a machine.
74 He encourages members to express their ideas and opinions.
75 He gives information on how to do things.

APPENDIX A

76 He calls members by their first names.
77 He puts group welfare above the welfare of any member.
78 He gives credit when credit is due.
79 He tries to keep the group in good standing with those in higher authority.
80 He emphasizes the quality of work.

81 He resists changes in ways of doing things.
82 He budgets his time.
83 He follows the guidance of the group.
84 He asks to be informed on decisions made by members.
85 He looks out for the personal welfare of individual members.

86 He tries to stop rumors when they occur.
87 He "rides" the member who makes a mistake.
88 He reverses his stand when he meets outside opposition.
89 He advises members to take it easy.
90 He originates new approaches to problems.

91 He sees that members have the material they need to work with.
92 He lets others do their work the way they think best.
93 He provides means for members to communicate with each other.
94 He attends social events of the group.
95 He blames the same members when anything goes wrong.

96 He tells a member when he does a particularly good job.
97 He presents only his own point of view to outsiders.
98 He stresses being ahead of competing groups.
99 He encourages members to start new activities.
100 He shows members how each job fits into the total picture.

101 He refuses to explain his actions.
102 He is aware of conflicts when they occur in the group.
103 He draws a definite line between himself and the rest of the group.
104 He discourages individual criticism of group behavior.
105 He explains the reasons for criticisms.

106 He speaks favorably of the group when talking with outsiders.
107 He "needles" members for greater effort.
108 He is first in getting things started.
109 He uses a standard method of evaluating members.
110 He acts without consulting the group.

111 He gives advance notice of changes.
112 He associates with members regardless of their position.
113 He stresses the importance of high morale in the group.
114 He uses constructive criticism.
115 He backs up the members in their actions.

116 He is slow to accept new ideas.
117 He sees to it that the work of members is coordinated.
118 He decides in detail what shall be done and how it shall be done.
119 He takes time to find out what members are doing.
120 He treats all members as his equal.

121 He helps members of the group settle their conflicts.
122 He criticizes a specific act rather than a person.
123 He contacts important people in an effort to help the group.
124 He is willing to make changes.
125 He stresses orderly methods of doing the job.

126 He invites criticism of his acts.
127 He makes members feel at ease when talking with him.
128 He is friendly and approachable.
129 He discourages members from pursuing their individual aims.
130 He uses his influence with outsiders in the interest of the group.

131 He schedules the work to be done.
132 He puts suggestions by the group into operation.
133 He knows about it when something goes wrong.
134 He pits one member against another.
135 He publicizes outstanding work of members of his group.

136 He emphasizes meeting of deadlines.
137 He regards what members do outside the group as of no concern to him.
138 He lets members know how they are doing.
139 He carries out the promises he makes.
140 He encourages the use of certain uniform procedures.

141 He gets group approval on minor matters before going ahead.
142 He knows who is responsible for each job.
143 He gets group approval on important matters before going ahead.
144 He reports progress to the group.
145 He lets the group set it own goals.

146 He keeps informed on how members think and feel about things.
147 He reports what is going on outside the group.
148 He makes sure his part in the group is understood by members.
149 He lets members know what is expected of them.
150 He tries to keep things as they are.

APPENDIX B

Item Analysis Data for 150 Items
of the Leader Behavior Description Questionnaire

Item Number

Dimension to Which the Item was Assigned

Scoring

    Form (Alternative Answer Scheme)

    Key (Scoring Direction:
          +2 to —2 or —2 to +2)

Correlation of Item with

    Own Dimension Total Score for
        Description by Others (Subordinates)
        Description by Self

    Highest Correlation with Other Dimensions for
        Descriptions by Others (Subordinates)
        Descriptions by Self

Correlation of Item with Leadership Evaluation for
        Descriptions by Others (Subordinates)
        Descriptions by Self

APPENDIX B
Item Analysis Data for 150 Items

Item Number	Dimension	Scoring Form	Key	Correlation with: Own Dimension Others	Correlation with: Own Dimension Self	Correlation with: Other Dimensions Others	Correlation with: Other Dimensions Self	Correlation with Evaluation Others	Correlation with Evaluation Self
				r	r	r	r	r	r
1	Organization	A	+	.70	.45	.45	.45	.60	.21
2	Domination	A	+	.40	.15	.50	.24	—.20	.22
3	Communication Down	A	+	.54	.70	.51	.68	.27	.10
4	Membership	B	+	.65	.49	.50	.37	.26	.23
5	Integration	C	+	.77	.62	.75	.56	.47	.11
6	Recognition	A	+	.80	.58	.67	.31	.40	.00
7	Representation	A	+	.62	.60	.47	.38	.38	.35
8	Production	C	+	.39	.50	.10	.37	—.10	.05
9	Initiation	B	+	.33	.47	.21	.43	.22	.22
10	Organization	A	+	.78	.48	.69	.33	.53	.42
11	Domination	A	+	.60	.64	.47	.37	.14	.13
12	Communication Up	B	+	.72	.40	.67	.40	.49	.00
13	Membership	B	+	.57	.54	.57	.43	.33	.23
14	Integration	B	+	.80	.66	.79	.47	.75	.25
15	Recognition	A	+	.07	.29	.63	.50	.02	.27
16	Representation	B	+	.60	.60	.51	.50	.48	.20
17	Production	C	+	.78	.42	.25	.29	.03	.10
18	Initiation	C	+	.63	.64	.49	.42	.41	.11
19	Organization	A	+	.33	.38	.40	.28	.04	—.05
20	Domination	A	+	.27	.59	.50	.59	.18	.10
21	Communication Down	A	+	.64	.38	.63	.41	.47	.38
22	Membership	C	+	.58	.35	.30	.30	.29	—.04
23	Integration	A	—	—.50	—.44	—.48	—.20	—.38	—.10
24	Recognition	B	+	.74	.51	.68	.31	.48	.05
25	Membership	C	+	.83	.51	.60	.63	.39	.29
26	Production	B	+	.83	.47	.25	.31	—.06	—.09
27	Initiation	A	—	—.35	—.30	.57	.34	.15	.10
28	Organization	A	—	—.43	—.62	—.45	—.37	—.42	.08
29	Domination	C	+	.64	.83	.47	.49	—.03	—.06
30	Communication Up	A	+	.81	.57	.73	.40	.42	.04
31	Membership	B	+	.58	.37	.70	.52	.60	.21
32	Integration	A	+	.75	.53	.75	.53	.50	.23
33	Recognition	B	+	—.03	—.14	.42	.54	—.30	—.16
34	Representation	A	+	.80	.50	.73	.35	.51	.15
35	Production	B	+	.66	.70	.62	.62	.17	.32
36	Initiation	A	—	.00	—.35	.10	.24	.12	—.31
37	Organization	A	+	.50	.60	.40	.40	.06	.10
38	Domination	A	+	.40	.74	.49	.27	—.33	—.10
39	Communication Down	A	+	.70	.73	.62	.57	.38	.19
40	Membership	A	+	.57	.68	.67	.38	.21	.25

Item Analysis Data for 150 Items—Continued

Item Number	Dimension	Scoring Form	Key	Correlation with: Own Dimension Others	Correlation with: Own Dimension Self	Correlation with: Other Dimensions Others	Correlation with: Other Dimensions Self	Correlation with Evaluation Others	Correlation with Evaluation Self
				r	r	r	r	r	r
41	Integration	B	+	.28	.37	.37	.37	.23	.03
42	Recognition	A	+	.80	.74	.74	.54	.52	.15
43	Representation	B	+	.75	.60	.63	.38	.44	.15
44	Production	A	+	.23	.50	.74	.46	.30	.52
45	Initiation	C	+	.75	.68	.59	.39	.48	.20
46	Organization	A	+	.71	.45	.55	.41	.16	.10
47	Domination	B	—	—.60	—.40	.58	.50	.21	.14
48	Communication Up	A	+	.68	.72	.67	.56	.29	.05
49	Membership	A	+	.65	.42	.29	.25	—.10	—.07
50	Integration	B	+	.50	.44	.57	.48	.28	—.13
51	Recognition	B	—	—.28	.10	.57	.51	—.05	—.10
52	Representation	B	+	.56	.35	.46	.39	.24	—.11
53	Production	A	+	.81	.53	.55	.49	.30	.05
54	Initiation	A	+	.59	—.42	.55	.31	.29	—.30
55	Organization	A	+	.71	.63	.52	.51	.45	.24
56	Domination	A	—	—.84	—.53	.82	.40	.45	—.16
57	Communication Down	B	+	.80	.39	.75	.39	.53	.17
58	Membership	B	+	.24	.48	.15	.17	—.10	—.10
59	Integration	C	+	.77	.52	.68	.56	.58	—.05
60	Recognition	A	+	.34	.29	.50	.45	.34	.23
61	Representation	A	+	.51	.52	.63	.44	.32	.05
62	Production	C	+	.55	.56	.27	.35	—.09	.24
63	Initiation	B	+	.77	.36	.67	.48	.44	.07
64	Organization	A	+	.79	.70	.70	.47	.47	.11
65	Domination	B	+	.79	.62	.25	.52	—.47	.05
66	Communication Up	A	+	.82	.83	.65	.83	.56	.13
67	Membership	C	—	—.67	—.51	—.42	—.32	—.26	—.11
68	Integration	A	+	.70	.72	.70	.58	.44	.10
69	Recognition	B	+	.48	.31	.53	.39	.30	—.17
70	Representation	A	+	.30	.50	.42	.30	.23	.10
71	Production	A	+	—.60	—.43	—.39	—.29	—.07	.11
72	Initiation	B	+	.79	.54	.62	.54	.47	.22
73	Organization	A	+	—.03	.28	.67	.55	—.39	.03
74	Domination	A	—	—.81	—.60	.81	.53	.58	.00
75	Communication Down	A	+	.54	.46	.62	.41	.33	.21
76	Membership	A	+	.58	.44	.29	—.31	—.03	—.20
77	Integration	A	+	.39	.36	.49	.36	.39	.00
78	Recognition	A	+	.88	.67	.76	.52	.48	.26
79	Representation	A	+	.66	.34	.65	.45	.29	.06
80	Production	B	+	.68	.55	—.59	.58	.32	—.22

Item Analysis Data for 150 Items—Continued

Item Number	Dimension	Scoring Form	Key	Correlation with: Own Dimension Others	Own Dimension Self	Other Dimensions Others	Other Dimensions Self	Correlation with Evaluation Others	Correlation with Evaluation Self
				r	r	r	r	r	r
81	Initiation	C	—	—.65	—.44	.57	.71	—.21	.01
82	Organization	A	+	.65	.60	.49	.48	.50	.26
83	Domination	A	—	—.73	—.58	.57	.39	.39	.25
84	Communication Up	A	+	.67	.69	.55	.48	.22	.15
85	Membership	A	+	.64	.48	.67	.36	.54	.06
86	Integration	A	+	.84	.68	.69	.71	.37	.13
87	Recognition	B	+	—.20	.00	—.40	.48	—.19	—.23
88	Representation	A	—	—.54	—.23	—.44	—.19	—.41	—.27
89	Production	B	—	—.25	—.13	.35	.32	.04	.10
90	Initiation	B	+	.89	.48	.70	.40	.53	.46
91	Organization	A	+	.56	.54	.54	.47	.23	.02
92	Domination	A	—	—.54	—.56	.39	—.37	.19	.00
93	Communication Down	A	+	.79	.32	.63	.23	.34	.18
94	Membership	A	+	.56	.46	—.68	—.40	.33	—.09
95	Integration	B	—	—.42	—.37	.56	.49	—.35	—.30
96	Recognition	A	+	.79	.83	.84	.46	.64	.18
97	Representation	A	—	—.21	—.44	.49	—.44	—.34	.31
98	Production	C	+	.57	.69	.53	.40	.11	—.01
99	Initiation	C	+	.79	.35	.68	.35	.30	.00
100	Organization	B	+	.73	.58	.74	.61	.44	.29
101	Domination	B	+	—.04	.47	—.47	—.40	.05	—.10
102	Communication Up	A	+	.72	.49	.72	.35	.50	.01
103	Membership	A	—	—.78	—.55	.80	.71	—.40	—.19
104	Integration	A	+	.17	.43	.20	.25	.10	.16
105	Recognition	A	+	.77	.63	.74	.48	.44	.02
106	Representation	A	+	.77	.73	.70	.50	.25	.29
107	Production	C	+	.64	.53	.48	.45	—.19	—.10
108	Initiation	A	+	.50	.17	.63	.38	.37	.31
109	Organization	A	+	.63	.39	.43	.50	.26	.04
110	Domination	B	+	.66	.52	—.58	—.41	—.13	—.13
111	Communication Down	A	+	.60	.49	—.80	.42	.54	.09
112	Membership	C	+	.60	.56	—.54	.48	.27	—.06
113	Integration	B	+	.84	.58	.69	.50	.47	.25
114	Recognition	A	+	.74	.53	.80	.63	.68	.34
115	Representation	A	+	.79	.47	.78	.38	.47	.06
116	Initiation	A	—	—.81	—.29	.67	.31	—.53	.08
117	Organization	A	+	.80	.74	.85	.54	.53	.09
118	Domination	A	+	.27	.46	.49	.46	—.08	—.05
119	Communication Up	A	+	.89	.63	.63	.58	.59	.07
120	Membership	A	+	.81	.64	—.79	—.54	.36	.11

Item Analysis Data for 150 Items—Continued

Item Number	Dimension	Scoring Form	Key	Correlation with: Own Dimension Others	Correlation with: Own Dimension Self	Correlation with: Other Dimensions Others	Correlation with: Other Dimensions Self	Correlation with Evaluation Others	Correlation with Evaluation Self
				r	r	r	r	r	r
121	Integration	A	+	.69	.39	.66	.48	.46	.22
122	Recognition	A	+	.53	.38	.46	.38	.27	.12
123	Representation	B	+	.92	.61	.80	.47	.57	.11
124	Initiation	A	+	.84	.68	—.72	.28	.55	.20
125	Organization	C	+	.70	.69	.70	.63	.54	.27
126	Domination	A	—	—.76	—.60	.77	.54	.57	—.09
127	Communication Down	A	+	.64	.31	.80	.44	.57	.18
128	Membership	A	+	.78	.48	.69	.60	.49	.19
129	Integration	A	+	.12	.18	—.23	.32	—.25	.03
130	Representation	B	+	.87	.78	.80	.55	.51	.35
131	Organization	A	+	.84	.54	.50	.54	.25	.39
132	Domination	A	—	—.87	—.62	.76	.76	.56	.30
133	Communication Down	A	+	.74	.64	.73	.49	.59	.29
134	Integration	B	—	—.53	—.29	.60	.64	—.35	—.16
135	Representation	B	+	.77	.60	.82	.55	.61	.13
136	Organization	C	+	.70	.64	.61	.43	.40	.20
137	Domination	B	—	—.06	—.20	—.18	—.23	—.18	.14
138	Communication Down	B	+	.78	.58	.81	.39	.57	.14
139	Integration	A	+	.64	.23	.70	.47	.48	.31
140	Organization	B	+	.70	.77	.51	.46	.39	.21
141	Domination	A	—	—.63	—.23	.50	.27	.14	—.03
142	Communication Up	A	+	.74	.62	.61	.62	.52	.20
143	Domination	A	—	—.88	—.74	.71	.40	.38	—.08
144	Communication Down	B	+	.79	.76	.74	.52	.41	.08
145	Domination	B	—	—.67	—.70	.60	.31	.20	.05
146	Communication Up	A	+	.89	.66	.86	.66	.65	.13
147	Communication Down	B	+	.80	.74	.79	.50	.51	.14
148	Communication Down	A	+	.56	.77	.55	.51	.40	.03
149	Communication Down	A	+	.67	.70	.61	.68	.43	.08
150	Initiation	B	—	—.26	—.40	.18	.44	—.31	—.08

APPENDIX C

APPENDIX C

Monographs
in the
Leadership Series in Ohio Studies in Personnel

Published in Cooperation With
The Personnel Research Board

Bureau of Business Research Monographs

R-80 *Methods in the Study of Administrative Leadership,*
by Ralph M. Stogdill, and Carroll L. Shartle

This monograph consists of a set of manuals which describe various methods that were developed for use in the Ohio State Leadership Studies. The methods include interviews, measures of organization structure, sociometric measures of personal interaction, measures of work performance, responsibility, authority, delegation and leader behavior, and ratings of effectiveness. Data on the reliability and validity of the various methods, and directions for administration and scoring the various tests and scales are included.

R-81 *Patterns of Administrative Performance,*
by Ralph M. Stogdill, Carroll L. Shartle and Associates

The four studies included in this monograph attempt to answer questions concerning the relationship of performance to the type of position occupied by the administrator. The methods used for the collection of data are those described in Monograph No. R-80. The data are analyzed in terms of differences between persons, between types of positions, between types of organizations and between levels (status) in the organization hierarchy.

R-82 *Leadership and Perceptions of Organization,*
by Ellis L. Scott

In this study of enlisted men aboard submarines, each man's perception of the structure of his unit or organization was compared with an organization chart prepared for his unit. The data are analyzed in terms of (1) discrepancies between perceived organization and charted organization, and (2) correspondences (reciprocations) between the perceptions of superiors, peers and subordinates. The relationship of perceptual error and perceptual reciprocation to morale, unit effectiveness and other variables is discussed. The methods used are based, in part, on those described in Monograph No. R-80.

R-83 *Leadership and Its Effects upon the Group,*
by Donald T. Campbell

This monograph, based on the study of a squadron of submarines, is concerned with the effects of leadership upon group performance and morale. A wide variety of criterion scores, including some 60 measures of effectiveness and morale for ships and for units of organization within ships, are analyzed and related to measures of leadership among commissioned and non-commissioned personnel. The criterion scores include objective measures as well as reputational data and evaluative ratings. The methods are based in part on those described in Monograph R-80.

R-84 *Leadership and Structure of Personal Interaction,*
by Ralph M. Stogdill

This monograph describes (1) a sociometric study of personal interaction in organizations of various sizes, and (2) a study of responsibility-authority relationships between superiors and subordinates in large and small organizations. Data on the relation of interaction measures and of responsibility and authority scores to measures of status, leader behavior and other variables are presented. Analysis of the data indicate that the performances, interactions, responsibility and authority of superiors exert a direct effect upon the performances and interactions of subordinates.

R-85 *A Predictive Study of Administrative Work Patterns,*
by Ralph M. Stogdill, Carroll L. Shartle, Ellis L. Scott,
Alvin E. Coons and William E. Jaynes

Twenty Navy officers were studied before being transferred to new positions. The twenty officers whom the transferees were to replace were also studied. The data obtained from the study of these two sets of officers were used to predict the future behavior of the officers being transferred. Six months later they were restudied on their new jobs. It was found that some forms of behavior were predicted more accurately in terms of the previous behavior of the men being transferred. Other behaviors were predicted more accurately in terms of the behavior of the previous occupants of the jobs. The methods for collecting data are described in Monograph No. R-80.

R-86 *Leadership and Role Expections*
by Ralph M. Stogdill, Ellis L. Scott, and William E. Jaynes

In this study of a large research organization, 57 civilian and military administrators were asked to describe what they do and what they ought to do on 45 items of work performance, leader behavior, responsibility and authority. The "does" and "ought to do" behaviors of each subject were also described by two subordinates. The data are analyzed in terms of relationships between expectations and performance, as well as in terms of discrepancies between expectations and performance. The methods for collecting data are described in Monograph R–80.

R–87 *Group Dimensions: A Manual for Their Measurement,*
by John K. Hemphill

This monograph describes a set of scales for the measurement of thirteen different dimensions of social groups. Normative data derived from the study of a wide variety of groups, as well as data on the reliability and validity of the scales are presented. The instructions include directions for administration and scoring. Data on the relation of group dimension scores to measures of productivity and job satisfaction are presented.

R–88 *Leader Behavior: Its Description and Measurement,*
by Ralph M. Stogdill and Alvin E. Coons, Editors

This monograph consists of a collection of papers by staff members of the Ohio State Leadership Studies. The papers describe the development, analysis and application of a set of items devised for the description of leader behavior. These items were used for the description of the leader behavior of business executives, foremen, teachers, college administrators, Air Force officers and Navy officers. Data on the relation of leader behavior to effectiveness measures, group descriptions and attitude climate are presented. A copy of the Leader Behavior Descriptions Questionnaire and directions for its use are also included.

Bureau of Educational Research Monographs

No. 32 *Situational Factors in Leadership,*
by John K. Hemphill, 1949, 144 pp.

This monograph presents the results obtained from a questionnaire study of 500 groups and their leaders. Each group was described by a member who checked scaled statements designed to describe 15 different group dimensions. The same Member also described the behavior and evaluated the adequacy of the top leader of the group. The data are analyzed in terms of the interrelationships between leader behavior, leadership adequacy and group dimensions.

No. 33 *Leadership and Supervision in Industry: An Evaluation of a Supervisory Training Porgram,*
   by Edwin A. Fleishman, Edwin F. Harris, and Harold E. Burtt, 1955, 110 pp.

   This monograph describes a study designed to evaluate the results of a training program for foremen in a large manufacturing plant. The subjects were three matched groups of foremen who had completed the human relations training course at different times, and a matched group of untrained foremen. The subjects described their own attitudes about how groups should be supervised and also described the behavior of their own supervisors. The superior and the subordinates of each foreman also described the behavior of the foreman and indicated their conception of the behavior of an ideal foreman. The analysis compares trained and untrained foremen, and compares the behavior, attitudes and effectiveness of foremen who operate under different patterns of leadership.